Sports Law in Greece

Sports Law in Greece

Achilleas Mavromatis

This book was originally published as a monograph in the International Encyclopaedia of Laws/Sports Law.

Founding Editor: Roger Blanpain
General Editor: Frank Hendrickx
Volume Editor: Michele Colucci

Wolters Kluwer

Published by:
Kluwer Law International B.V.
PO Box 316
2400 AH Alphen aan den Rijn
The Netherlands
E-mail: lrs-sales@wolterskluwer.com
Website: www.wolterskluwer.com/en/solutions/kluwerlawinternational

Sold and distributed by:
Wolters Kluwer Legal & Regulatory U.S.
920 Links Avenue
Landisville, PA 17538
United States of America
E-mail: customer.service@wolterskluwer.com

ISBN 978-94-035-2418-4

e-Book: ISBN 978-94-035-2428-3
web-PDF: ISBN 978-94-035-2438-2

The Author

Dr Achilleas Mavromatis is a lawyer and member of the Mavromatis Law Office which is located in Thessaloniki, Greece. He graduated from the Law School of Aristotle University of Thessaloniki, Greece, where he also obtained a master's degree in Penal Law and Criminology and a PhD in Sports Penal Law after the defence of his work titled 'Sport Crimes in Greece'.

Sports Law is his main field of activity, both on a scientific and a practical level. He was member of the Foundation Board of the 'World Anti-Doping Agency (WADA)', representing the Greek Minister of Culture Dr E. Venizelos (2003), member of the Greek National Anti-Doping Organization ('ESKAN – National Council Against Doping' 2003–2006), member of the Commission for the Preparation of the Greek Presidency in European Union (EU) (2002–2003), Secretary of the Legal Commission of the 'European Volleyball Confederation' (CEV 2001–2011 – member 1995–2001), Chairman of the 'First Degree Commission for the Resolution of Financial Differences of Professional Volleyball Players' of the Hellenic Volleyball Federation (1994–2004), Chairman, of the 'Legal Commission of the Hellenic Volleyball Federation' (1993–2004), member of the 'Law-preparatory and Law-technical Committee', constituted at the General Secretariat of Sports for the preparation and voting by the Greek Parliament of Law 3057/2002 (2002) and Law 3207/2003 (2003), President of the Hellenic Volleyball Federation (2010–2016), member of the Hellenic Olympic Committee (HOC) (2013–2016), member of the Board of Administration of the 'International Volleyball Federation' (FIVB) seated in Lausanne (2016–2020) and member of the Board of Administration of the 'European Volleyball Confederation' (CEV) seated in Luxemburg (2011–2020). Today, he is Head of the Legal Department of PAOK FC (since 2008) and Court of Arbitration for Sport (CAS) Arbitrator (since 2023).

He has been since 2018 giving lectures in Sports Law in the Post Graduate Degree of Sports Management of the School of Physical Education and Sports Science of Thessaloniki as well as in other Universities, has published and cooperated in the publication of several books concerning sports law, has written scientific articles and has participated in several congresses, presenting speeches referring to sports law issues.

The Author

Special thanks to my colleagues Iraklis Tsiarapas, George Rodinos, Konstantinos Georgiou and Paraskevi Efthimiadi for their contribution as well as to my children Kalliopi and Socrates for the inspiration and support.

Table of Contents

Table of Contents

List of Abbreviations

Adm. Just.	Administrative Justice (Scientific Magazine)
AAE	Anonimi Athlitiki Eteria (Sport Limited Company)
Arm.	Armenopoulos (Scientific Magazine)
ASEAD	Anotato Simvulio Epilisis Athitikon Diaforon (Supreme Council for the Settlement of Sport Disputes)
CAS	Court of Arbitration for Sport
CC	Civil Code
DEAV	Diarkis Epitropi Antimetopisis tis Vias (Permanent Committee for the Confrontation of Sport Violence)
Def.	Defence (Scientific Magazine)
DEN	Deltio Ergatikis Nomothesias (Scientific Magazine)
EC	Executive Committee
ECJ	European Court of Justice
EEA	Epitropi Epaggelmatikou Athlitismou (Committee of Professional Sport)
EEODAK	Epitropi Epilisis Athlitikon Diaforon Amivomenon Kalathosferiston (Committee for the Resolution of Disputes of Paid Basketball Players)
EFIP	Epitropi Filathlou Pnevmatos (Committee of Sport Spirit)
EFIPID	Epitropi Filathlou Pnevmatos Ithikis kai Deontlogias (Philatelic Sports Spirit, Ethics and Deontology Committee)
EFKA	Ethnikos Foreas Koinonikis Asfalisis (National Social Security Agency)
EKEAD	Elliniko Kentro Erevnas Athitikou Dikeou (Greek Centre of Research of Sport Law)
EllEpEgl	Elliniki Epitheorisi Eglimatologias (Greek Review of Criminology – Scientific Magazine)
EOE	Elliniki Olimpiaki Epitropi (Greek Olympic Committee)
EOK	Hellenic Basketball Federation
EPO	Elliniki Omospondia Podosferou (Greek Football Federation)

List of Abbreviations

ESAP	Enosi Somation Amivomenon Petosferiston (Union of Associations of Paid Volleyball Athletes)
ESAKE	Enosi Kalathosfaerikon Anonimon Eterion (Union of Basketball Limited Companies)
ESKAN	National Council for Combatting Doping
EOKAN	Ethnikos Organismos Katapolemisis Doping (National Organization for Combatting Doping)
EU	European Union
FIFA	Federation International des Football Associations
HFF	Hellenic Football Federation
HGC	Hellenic Gaming Commission
HOC	Hellenic Olympic Committee
IASL	International Association of Sports Law
IOC	International Olympic Committee
KAE	Kalathosferiki Anonimi Eteria (Basketball Limited Company)
NoB	Nomiko Vima (Scientific Magazine)
OPAP	Organismos Prognostikon Agonon Podosferou (Organization of Prediction of Football Matches)
OTA	Local Self-Administration Organizations
PAE	Podosferiki Anonimi Eteria (Football Limited Company)
PC	Penal Code
PD	Presidential Decree
PenJust	Penal Justice (Scientific Magazine)
PinChron	Pinika Chronika (Penal Minutes-Scientific Magazine) publ Publications
Rev. Sp.L.	Revision of Sport Law (Scientific Magazine)
RNG	Random Number Generator
TAA	Tmimata Amivomenon Athliton (Sections of Paid Athletes)
UEFA	Union of European Football Associations
WADA	World Anti-doping Agency

General Introduction

Chapter 1. General Background

1. Sport is one of the major human activities in Greece as well as all over the world, having its roots in ancient Greece, where physical education was extremely important from a social and political point of view. The cornerstone of life in that era was the idea of the necessity for the simultaneous exercise of body and spirit. Sport activity in ancient times was not limited to exercise, but it involved competitions (organization of sport events, e.g., Olympic Games, Pythia, Isthmia, Nemea, etc.).

2. The success of the participants in the above games, especially in the Olympics, was considered to be of major importance, without the participation itself being underestimated. Proof of their major importance is the fact that during the Olympics, every war activity stopped (Olympic Truce).

3. Through their long-time operation, the principles of sport ideal and fair play were formed. The operation of these games was governed by certain rules for their faultless organization. These rules, which can be considered the first sports law rules in history, were implemented by several instruments, such as the Olympic Parliament.

4. The ancient Olympic Games lasted from 776 B.C. to 393 A.D. After several centuries with no special sport activity in Greece, at the end of the nineteenth century, physical education was included in the Greek educational system and the first sport clubs, under their form, were founded. The first modern Olympic Games, organized in Athens in 1896 spotlit the rebirth of sport in Greece. The most popular sports were football and track and field, but other sports were cultivated as well (swimming, wrestling, shooting, weight lifting, etc.).

5. The eruption of sport in modern Greece took place in the sixties and the seventies. In 1979, football was the first sport to obtain a professional league, followed by basketball and volleyball (in a semi-professional form) in the mid-1990s.

6. Today in Greece, sports are very popular, especially after the victories of the national Greek teams in the European Championships in basketball in 1987 and 2006 and in football in 2004 and the tremendous success of the Greek athletes in the Olympics held in Atlanta (1996), Sydney (2000) and Athens (2004). Since 2010, due to the financial crisis, sports have been seriously affected and have entered into a new modern era.

7. The scientific development of Sports Law, though, has not reached the same level. Only recently, efforts aiming to introduce it in all Law and Physical Education Universities become more intensive and specialized sports lawyers are dealing with the continuously increasing number of sports law cases.

Chapter 2. Sources of Sport Law

8. The Greek Constitution, the supreme national law, has provisions for both physical education and sports. It constitutes the major source of the sports law in Greece. Article 16, paragraph 2 stipulates physical education as one of the main missions of the State, the goal of which is the making of free and responsible citizens. Article 16, paragraph 9 makes provision for sport activity and establishes the role of the State in the protection, supervision and control of sport institutions.

9. The most important law for sport issues is law 2725/1999, which replaced the basic sports law of the last part of the twentieth century, 75/1975. Law 2725/1999 as modified by laws 2858/2000, 2947/2001, 3057/2002, 3207/2003, 3259/2004, 3262/2004, 3372/2005, 3472/2006, 3479/2006, 3708/2008, 4049/2012, 4115/2013, 4151/2013, 4229/2014, 4238/2014, 4282/2014, 4316/2014, 4326/2015, 4355/2015, 4373/2016, 4410/2016, 4429/2016, 4431/2016, 4446/2016, 4479/2017, 4587/2018, 4603/2019, 4612/2019, 4622/2019, 4625/2019, 4639/2019, 4700/2020, 4714/2020, 4722/2020, 4726/2020, 4734/2020, 4753/2020, 4763/2020, 4777/2021, 4778/2021, 4787/2021, 4809/2021, 4818/2021, 4831/2021, 4908/2022, 4934/2022, 4938/2022, 4964/2022, 4972/2022, 4975/2022, 4982/2022, 5025/2023, 5039/2023, 5043/2023, 5046/2023 and 5085/2024 sets a basis in the field of sport legislation as a result of the attempt to deal with sport issues in a unified way. Nowadays, law 2725/1999, in combination with the presidential and ministerial decrees issued according to its provisions, constitute the main source of law for both amateur and professional sport.

10. The continuous law-changing procedure, common in all legal life in Greece, especially during the financial crisis of the last decade, does not enable anyone who wants to study the existing legislation because, even though the basic structure of the main sports law has not changed, in many articles several amendments changed more than once the initial provision. Recently, the Minister of Sports announced an initiative to unify all existing law provisions for sport in a Sports Law Code, but such an effort will definitely need a long time to be realized. It seems though that what is really required is a new sports law covering sports as they function in modern society, which is much different than the one at the beginning of the century.

11. Apart from law 2725/1999, other laws and legal provisions, such as the Civil Code (CC), the commercial laws, the Penal Code (PC), etc., are also sources of sports law, to the extent that they deal with issues that do not need a special confrontation.

12. Another source of sports law is the international conventions, ratified by law, in order to be directly applied within the Greek legal system and the European Law. The European Union (EU) Treaty and its related documents, like the White Paper on Sport, play an important role, while the most important international conventions related to sports and ratified by the Greek Parliament are the European Convention against doping of the Council of Europe (Strasbourg, 1989), the new International Anti-Doping Convention agreed in the Headquarters of UNESCO, in

Paris in 2005 ratified with law 3516/2006, the International Convention for Violence (Strasbourg, 1985, ratified by law 1787/1988), the European Convention on the Manipulation of Sports Competitions of 18 September 2014 (Magglingen/Macolin Convention), ratified by law 4639/2019. and the European Convention of 3 July 2016 for integrated security, protection and access to services in football matches and other sports events, which has not yet been ratified by law.

13. The decisions of the courts are not considered as source of law in the Greek legal system. Nevertheless, the interpretation of the legislation can be seriously taken into consideration.

Chapter 3. Specificity of Sport

14. The concept of the specificity of sport is mentioned in several documents issued by the EU institutions. In the *Helsinki Report on Sport* (1999), it is affirmed that '*the application of the Treaty's competition rules to the sporting sector must take account of the specific characteristics of sport, especially the interdependence between sporting activity and the economic activity that it generates, the principle of equal opportunities and the uncertainty of the result*'. According to the *Declaration of Nice* (2000), '*even though not having any direct powers in this area, the Community must, in its action under the various Treaty provisions, take account of the social, educational and cultural functions inherent in sport and making it special, in order that the code of ethics and the solidarity essential to the preservation of its social role may be respected and nurtured*'.

15. However, neither the Nice Declaration nor the Helsinki Report contains a clear definition of the specificity of sport: the Helsinki Report simply lists some specific characteristics of sports activities that are particularly important in the field of antitrust law, whereas the Nice Declaration identifies the specificity of sport with the social, educational and cultural functions inherent in sport.

16. The same applies to the *White Paper on Sport* (2007), where it is stated that '*sport has certain* specific characteristics, *which are often referred to as the* "specificity of sport"'. According to the White Paper, the specificity of sport can be approached through two prisms: '*the specificity of sporting activities and of sporting rules, such as separate competitions for men and women, limitations on the number of participants in competitions, or the need to ensure uncertainty concerning outcomes and to preserve a competitive balance between clubs taking part in the same competitions; the specificity of the sport structure, including the autonomy and diversity of sport organisations, a pyramid structure of competitions from grassroots to elite level and organised solidarity mechanisms between the different levels and operators, the organisation of sport on a national basis, and the principle of a single federation per sport*'.

17. This recognition of the specific nature of sport has been constitutionalized by the 2009 Treaty of Lisbon in the second paragraph of Article 165(1) and also in the seventh paragraph of Article 165(2) Treaty on the Functioning of the European Union (TFEU) which states that '*the Union shall contribute to the promotion of European sporting issues while taking account of the specific nature of sport*'. Again, the specificity of sport is only mentioned but not defined.

18. Lastly, the report Mapping the specificity of sport by the European Commission – Directorate-General for Education and Culture (2016) says that 'the specificity of sport refers to the inherent characteristics of sport which set it apart from other economic and social activities'.

19. It follows from the foregoing that under EU sports policy, all the institutions agree on the fact that sport is special in the sense that it is different from any other activity because of its social and educational dimension. That said, if one tries to translate this concept into a definition to be applied in concrete cases, it is impossible to find a common benchmark.

20. Greece is an EU Member State, and this means that EU legislation applies directly to all activities within Greece at a higher level than national legislation. Therefore, all the above may be considered part of the national law. The notion of specificity is not clear in the national legislation as well, but there are several examples of law treating sports activity in a different way than other ones. For example, any person with a certain criminal record may become a Board member in a commercial SA but may not become a Board member in a professional Anonimi Athlitiki Eteria (Sport Limited Company) (AAE). However, while the CC provides that a minimum of twenty persons are required to create an association, law 2725/1999 provides that ten clubs are enough to create a sport union (Article 11) and five unions are enough to create a sport federation (Article 20).

Part I. Organization of Sports

Chapter 1. Sports Governance

21. Good sports governance is absolutely necessary today due to the increasing importance of sport phenomenon in many aspects of social life and has been a very important issue within the EU as well as the major international sports organizations.

22. All sports governing bodies in Greece function within the framework of their legal personality (private or public) obtained according to the Greek legislation and supervised by the Greek State. The extent of the intervention of the State in sports activity is still under discussion, the more accepted opinion being that sport bodies may act independently only in clearly sport matters (rules of games, etc.).

23. Nevertheless, the role of sport governing bodies today goes far beyond the adoption of playing rules since sport is not only a social and cultural phenomenon but also a business. Both the Deputy Ministry of Sport and the competent regional institutions are responsible to control that sport associations, unions or federations function in a way that is compatible with the main goal of the sport activity, as it is foreseen by the law and within the legal provisions set for this reason.

24. The development of sports and the necessity of good governance due to the growing financial impact of the sports activity led to the development of the science of sports management.

§1. Governmental Institutions and Bodies

25. The Greek Constitution itself defines in Article 16, paragraph 9, that sport lies under the protection and the supreme supervision of the State. This article mainly covers the intervention of the legislator in the sport activity to protect it and supervise it as an activity of public interest. In many cases, though, the intervention of the legislator exceeds the expected level and unjustifiably restricts the autonomy of sport as it is recognized by sports law scientists globally.

26. Until 2023, there was no separate Ministry of Sport in Greece, but a Deputy Minister of Sport functioned under the auspices of the Minister of Culture and Sports. Since 2023, the Deputy Minister of Sports has functioned in the Ministry of

Education (https://www.minedu.gov.gr/). The organization, the protection institutions and the supervision of sport belong to the competence of the Deputy Minister of Sport and the General Secretary of Sport.

27. The General Secretariat of Sport (www.gga.gov.gr) is the main governmental body related to sports. Its Head is the General Secretary of Sport who becomes second in the hierarchy after the Deputy Minister of Sport. The competence and the responsibilities of the General Secretariat of Sport are defined by the ministerial decree in Official Gazette 28A/1.3.1985 and Presidential Decree (PD) 4/2018.

28. As foreseen in the law 2725/1999, the General Secretariat of Sport has the responsibility for (i) the organization and function of various commissions such as the Permanent Committee for the Confrontation of Sport Violence (DEAV), the Committee of Professional Sports (EEAs), the Supreme Council for the Settlement of Sport Disputes (ASEAD), the Committee of International Sports Relations, or departments such as the Directorate of Sport for All, Promotion, Sports Development, Scientific Support and International Relations functioning within its frame, as well as for (ii) the supervision of other institutions established with provisions of the sports law without legal personality, such as the National Center of Sports Research or with legal personality, such as the National Organization for Combatting Doping (EOKAN), the Hellenic Olympic Committee (HOC), the International Olympic Academy, the National Paralympic Committee, the National Sports Federation for Disabled, and all sports federations, unions and associations in the country.

29. The DEAV is foreseen in Article 41A of law 2725/1999, as it has been modified several times so far (last with the law 5085/2024) consisting of its President, Vice-President and three members as follows: one retired supreme judge or prosecutor, two scientists of law specialized in criminal or sports law, one supreme police officer, and one employee of GGA. It has among other the following goals: to cooperate with the organizers of sports events, to support police and to give opinion for the evaluation of risk of sports events, to propose to the Minister of Sport the prohibition of selling tickets to away team fans and the possible postponement of a sports event for security reasons, to survey the application of laws and regulations concerning the confrontation of sport violence and the editing of a relevant annual report which is submitted to the General Secretariat of Sport, to make a report and suggestions to the Minister after the end of each season for the rewarding (either material or moral) of sport associations, unions or even athletes that have shown ideal athletic behaviour and to impose administrative sanctions or propose to the Minister the imposition of administrative sanctions according to Articles 41B, 41Γ, 41Δ and 41E of law 2725/1999 and 1 and 1A of law 4326/2015. Law 5085/2024 introduced in application of the Convention of Saint Denis the creation of a National Steering Committee, composed by representatives of governmental and sports institutions with some of the old competences of DEAV, such as proposals to the Minister of Sport for law amendments, control of the efficiency of the existing laws, information of the public, etc.

30. The EEAs is constituted according to the provisions of Article 77 of law 2725/1999. It was first included in the law with the amendment of the law 3057/2002, which has been amended several times so far. It is composed of seven members and seven substitute members as follows: One retired Supreme Court judge or prosecutor as Chairman, one professor of sports management or commercial or public law, one lawyer specialized in companies' law, one lawyer specialized in sports law, one economist and two members with experience in sports. Persons having served in the past years as members of the government or sports executives or professionally connected with AAEs or clubs or as referees, coaches, athletes, etc., may not be appointed as members of the EEA. The main task of EEA is to control the AAEs and all legal or natural persons involved in their activity in legal and financial matters, issue licences for obtaining shares in the AAEs, issue certificates at the beginning of every season for the participation of companies in the professional championships and impose sanctions or refer any breach of law to the competent disciplinary organs or criminal courts.

31. The ASEAD functions according to the provisions of Articles 123 et seq. of law 2725/1999 as the second-grade disciplinary and jurisdictional organ for all sports except football. It is composed of fifteen members, all judges of civil and administrative courts and prosecutors appointed by the administration of the respective courts of Athens with a two-year term of office. A.S.E.A.D. operates in three sections and a Plenary Session. The composition of the departments is determined by its president. Each department meets with a five-member composition. Exceptionally, when the judging department of A.S.E.A.D. considers that the case is of major importance, he can refer it to the Plenary Session. Duties of secretaries of A.S.E.A.D. are performed by permanent employees of the G.G.A., appointed by the General Secretary of Sports. In Thessaloniki, there is a special local section of the A.S.E.A.D.

32. The Committee for International Sports Relations (Article 42 law 2725/1999) has the mission to promote the international relations and cooperation of the Ministry with the international sports community and is composed of the General Secretary of Sport, one representative of the Ministry of Foreign Affairs, one employee of the General Secretariat of Sport and two other members appointed by the Deputy Minister of Sport.

33. The National Committee of School Sport and Olympic Education is constituted by Ministerial Degree with advisory and coordinative role regarding the school sports.

34. The Directorate of Sport for All, Promotion, Sports Development, Scientific Support and International Relations (Article 39 of law 2725/1999) is competent for the organization, implementation, supervision, and support of all Programmes and Events for Sport for All. These Programmes and Events address all citizens aiming to improve the level of their health and wellness, the cultivation of sports conscience, the utilization of free time and the recreation of all citizens. They are implemented in cooperation with local government organizations and sports entities, like federations, unions, associations, etc. The General Secretariat of Sport may financially contribute to these Programmes and Events.

35. The sport law in Article 39, paragraph 1 had established a legal entity of private law with the title of Institution for Mass Sport. This institution, set out by law 3057/2002, never functioned, and it was replaced with the Directorate of Sport for All, Promotion, Sports Development, Scientific Support and International Relations within the gulfs of the General Secretariat of Sports.

36. Law 2725/1999 also provided the establishment of the National Council of Sport Planning (Article 40) and the Committee for the Information of the International Sport Institutions are sport institutions foreseen in law 2725/1999 (Article 42), which were never activated. Article 40 has been abolished by Article 29 of law 4373/2016, and Article 42 has been replaced by Article 30 of law 4373/2016, foreseeing the creation of the Committee of International Sports Relations.

37. The National Center of Sport Research is located in the Athens Olympic Stadium. Its goal is the promotion of research, the development of the sport-related sciences, the exploitation of results of the research, as well as the collection and distribution of information of scientific and technological interest for sport issues. In law 2725/1999 (Article 38), it is foreseen to be replaced by the Greek Centre for Sport Research and Technology, which will additionally have educational competence, especially for the education of coaches, but so far, this has not taken place.

38. Beyond the abovementioned committees, law foresees and also provides the creation of organizing and executive committees (ECs) (Article 53, paragraphs 1–4 of law 2725/1999) upon the decision of the competent deputy minister, which functions under the auspices of the General Secretariat for Sports. These committees have the responsibility to carry out the organization of main sport events and the creation and elaboration of the laws relevant to sport issues, as well as to introduce and execute programs for the promotion of the sport and Olympic education. They may obtain legal personality as provided in the Ministerial Decree of their creation.

39. The EOKAN (www.eokan.gr) replaced the National Council for Combatting Doping (ESKAN), which had been established as a Committee of the Ministry of Sport with Article 128F of law 2725/1999, added with Article 57 of law 3057/2002 and replaced with Article 18 of law 3708/2008. Article 11 of law 4049/2012, amended with Article 123 of law 4446/2016, changed ESKAN's name to EOKAN and its legal status to obtain legal personality. This change was only put into effect some years later, in 2022, with the issuance of the PD 87/2020 providing all details for the change in the legal status and the function of the national anti-doping organization. For international relations, the name E.O.K.A.N. is rendered in the English language as the 'Hellenic Anti-doping Agency (H.ADA)'. EOKAN is seated in the Region of Attica.

40. The administrative bodies of E.O.K.A.N. are the Board of Directors (BoD) and he Governor, who chairs the Board of Directors. The Board of Directors of

E.O.K.A.N. consists of nine members and is set up according to the provisions of Article 5 of the PD 87/2020 by decision of the competent Minister of Sports, as follows: (a) Three members are specialist scientists from the field of medicine or pharmacology or toxicology or of biology or chemistry or biochemistry with knowledge in dealing with doping, one of whom is selected from a list of at least five candidates, submitted by the Board of Directors of the Panhellenic Medical Association, (b) Three members are lawyers with experience in sports and anti-doping matters, (c) One member of the Plenary of the Hellenic Paralympic Committee, indicated by it, (d) One member of the Plenary of the HOC, indicated by it, (e) One member of the Teaching Research Staff of the Schools of Science of Physical Education and Sports (S.E.F.A.A.), indicated from a list submitted by the Deans of the S.E.F.A.A. of A.E.I. The duties of the Secretary of the Board of Directors are exercised by an employee who serves in E.O.K.A.N. who is appointed together with his deputy by the decision of the Governor of E.O.K.A.N. The term of office of the members of the Board of Directors of E.O.K.A.N. is four years and is automatically extended until the appointment of a new Board of Directors, but not, however, for a period longer than six months from its expiry.

41. The Board of Directors of E.O.K.A.N. exercises according to Article 7 of the PD 87/2020 the following responsibilities: (a) Approves the general action policy of the E.O.K.A.N., drawn up by the Governor to fulfil its objectives. (b) Approves the long-term action plan, designed and submitted jointly by the Governor and the Executive Director. (c) Approves the Organization's budget submitted by the Financial Service for each financial year and the necessary amendments required during its execution. (d) Approves the ratification of all contracts concluded by the Organization with suppliers, after they have been signed by the Executive Director, in accordance with the applicable legislation of the EU on public contracts. (e) Proposes to the supervising Ministry, following a relevant recommendation of the Executive Director, the necessary legislative measures to achieve the goals of the EOKAN and improve its organization and operation in accordance with the Anti-Doping Code and the International Standards, as they are amended and in force. (f) Decides on the formation of permanent and extraordinary committees for the processing of scientific issues in the cases where this is required by the Code and International Standards. (g) Decides on every issue, which falls within the competence of the Governor, if the Governor decides to refer it to him for an opinion or a decision.

42. The EOKAN Governor is appointed by the decision of the Minister of Sports for a four-year term renewable only once and presides over the Board of Directors of EOKAN. The Governor has the following powers: (a) Manages the E.O.K.A.N., is in charge of all its Services and the personnel serving in them and supervises the execution of the decisions of the Board of Directors and all anti-doping program controls. (b) Convenes the Board of Directors, determines and recommends the items on the agenda and directs its meetings. (c) He is responsible for the execution of operating expenses within the limits of the annual approved budget. (d) Sign, after authorization of the Board of Directors, contracts concluded by E.O.K.A.N. with third parties. (e) Examines and recommends for approval to the Board of

Directors the annual and long-term action programme of E.O.K.A.N. in all areas, which has been prepared by the Executive Director. (f) Represents the Organization before any administrative or judicial authority as well as out of court, in Councils, Committees, Scientific conferences, events and seminars at national, European and international levels. The presiding Governor, absent or incapacitated, is replaced in all his duties by an advisor appointed by a decision of the Board of Directors.

43. The Governor and the Board of Directors members must not fall under the obstacles of civil servants according to the Civil Service Code (law 3528/2007) or must not have been convicted or referred by an irrevocable judicial will or summons in a trial for using prohibited substances and methods, violation of doping legislation, or have been disciplinary sanctioned for an anti-doping rule violation. They must not be members of the Board of Administration or shareholders of a AAE, members of a Sections of Paid Athletes (TAA), or members of the Board of Administration of a sports federation, and they must not provide their services to any of the above institutions. They must also not be active coaches, professional athletes or intermediaries.

44. E.O.K.A.N. has the following responsibilities: (a) Performs a risk analysis, draws up the program of all doping controls, allocates and selects the controls in the relevant sports during or outside the Games, orders doping control to the sampling services and assigns the analysis of the samples to a recognized by the World Anti-Doping Agency (WADA) laboratory, in accordance with the World Anti-Doping Code. (b) It is responsible for the education and training of those responsible for taking doping control samples (samplers) and for the procedures for the safe collection and transport of samples to a WADA recognized doping control laboratory. (c) It is responsible for managing the results of the tests in accordance with the World Anti-Doping Code and the WADA International Standards for the Management of Results. (d) Assigns a special committee to examine requests for the exception of the use of prohibited substances for therapeutic purposes in accordance with the World Anti-Doping Code. (e) Establishes a Primary Disciplinary Committee in accordance with the provisions of the law. (f) Draws up, promotes and implements independently or in collaboration with sports federations and other sports bodies, education bodies and the media, educational information programs and information campaigns to prevent the use by athletes of prohibited substances and methods with emphasis on the health risks of doping and the damage it causes to the ethical values of sport. (g) Recommends to the Minister of Sports any measure aimed at preventing or combating the use of prohibited substances and methods. (h) Advises the Minister of Sports on any draft law or regulatory act regarding anti-doping measures. (i) Cooperates with the competent sports bodies, the competent authorities, the Greek Police, Interpol, the National Medicines Agency, the General Directorate of Customs and Excise and any other national or international body active in the fight against doping. (j) Draws up and submits to the Minister of Sports a report on its activities during the immediately preceding year, in which the action and results of its work and the planning of its upcoming activities are presented and analysed. This report is published on the website of E.O.K.A.N. and notified to the WADA. (k) It represents the country in the Committees of the Council of Europe, the WADA, and UNESCO, as well as in every other European and international Organization. (l) Develops any other activity and makes decisions on any other matter which are relevant to its responsibilities and purposes.

45. Apart from the above, governmental institutions should be considered, despite their private legal personality, the Councils of the major sports facilities which belong to the state, such as the Olympic Athletic Center of Athens (OAKA), the Peace and Friendship Stadium in Piraeus (SEF), etc.

46. Greek State used to offer considerable financial support to all sport governing bodies in Greece, the latter having to ensure that it is used for the purpose it is allocated for.

47. The General Secretariat of Sports, having the authority to administer part of the profits of Organization of Prediction of Football Matches (OPAP) and Organization of Horse Racing in Greece (ODIE), used to provide allocations to all amateur sport institutions including associations, unions and federations, under its supervision according to Articles 49 and 50 of the law 2725/1999. Those allocations intend to support the efforts of these institutions for the development of all sports, especially among young people, the organization of sport events and the participation in those, the confrontation of all necessary expenses for their proper function and the construction and conservation of sport facilities. Since 2010, when an unprecedented financial crisis hit Greece, only sports federations and stadiums received allocations from the State. It is only a decade later, in 2022, that Article 62 of law 4949/2022 amended Article 60 of law 2961/2001 providing that part of the profit of the taxation of the betting companies would be distributed to associations, unions, federations, AAEs, etc. With this provision, the State restarted after more than a decade to support the sports activity, although the initial reasoning for the above amendment was to cover the loss from the limited sport activity due to COVID-19.

48. Apart from other controls by the tax and other public authorities, which have been extremely intensive during the crisis period (since 2011), all sport institutions that have received any allocation from the State must submit to the General Secretariat of Sports a financial report for the amount allocated; otherwise, they cannot receive further allocations. Additionally, all sport institutions have the obligation according to Article 51 of the same law to render budget and account on an annual basis.

49. Article 52 of the law 2725/1999 provided that the Control Council of the General Secretariat of Sports, composed of sixteen employees of the General Secretariat of Sports and six employees of the Ministry of Finance, was the public authority that has the right to control sport institutions. All the sport institutions allocated by the State are subject to its control: (a) for the confirmation of compliance with the provisions regarding the managerial and the logistical rules of the sport law, (b) for compliance with the acts of the administration, and (c) for the fulfilment of their financial obligations, according to Article 52, paragraphs 1 and 2 of law 2725/

1999, as it was modified by Article 77 of law 3057/2002, Article 26 of law 3262/2004 and Article 18, paragraph 14 of law 3708/2008. A special provision for the exclusion of the private financial sources of the Hellenic Football Federation (HFF) from the above control, which was foreseen by Article 77 of law 3057/2002, was abolished by Article 46 of law 4373/2016.

50. Sport institutions were obliged to give any required information about the logistical books and documents to the Control Council. A denial to comply with this obligation had as a consequence, the restraint of the allocation from the General Secretariat of Sports for at least two months and in case of repetition for at least six months, following a confirmation of the Control Council (Article 52, paragraph 3).

51. The control takes place whenever, after the command of the Minister of Culture and Education. A copy of the control results is sent to the relevant judicial institution for the infliction of sanctions in case a violation of the law is found (Article 52, paragraphs 4 and 5). The abovementioned judicial instrument carries out an investigation for possible penal crimes. In case such crimes have been committed, the report of the results is sent to the competent public prosecutor, according to Article 52, paragraph 6 of law 2725/1999, as it has been modified by Article 77 of law 3057/2002. The control of the State over the sport institutions and especially sport federations has become stricter after 2011.

52. In 2019, law 4603/2019 changed this control structure by amending Article 52 and adding Article 52A and 52B as follows: The financial control of the sport institutions takes place in two levels:

(i) By the General Inspector of Public Administration, who can at his own discretion execute full management, logistic and financial control of any institution that has received in the previous year a total financial support exceeding EUR 50,000 or upon demand of the Deputy Minister of Sport to any institution regardless the amount of the received financial support. The Inspector has the right to control bank accounts and writes a report, which he submits to the Deputy Minister and, in case he considers that illegal actions took place, to the competent Prosecutor to initiate a criminal investigation. He may also propose the suspension of the financial support to this institution for a certain period of time. During the control by the Inspector, all administration members, athletes, coaches, employees, and co-operators of the institution are obliged to provide him any information asked as well as documents or other evidence. In case of delay or denial on purpose to provide to the Inspector any required document or evidence or submission of false evidence, a criminal prosecution may start against the responsible person, leading to a sanction of imprisonment of at least two years and a fine of more than EUR 10,000 unless a heavier sanction is provided for the same action in another law.

(ii) By the General Secretariat of Sport which may conduct on-site control in sports institutions to certify that the data registered in the Registry of Sports Institutions and the Registry of Sport Associations is accurate and that law provisions and obligations are fully applied and the regulations are respected during official competitions. It is obvious that especially the last (control of the respect of the regulations) exceeds the limits of acceptable intervention in the self-government of sports institutions. The above control is exercised by small groups of three employees of the General Secretariat of Sport. In case the data submitted in the Registry are false or breach of any law provision, the respective institution may be sanctioned by deletion from the Registry, recall of the Special Athletic Recognition or other administrative sanctions.

53. The control of the General Secretariat of Sports into sport institutions is exercised also by the approval of all the regulations of the federations submitted for control of their conformity with the legislation according to Article 27 of the law 2725/2999 and by the right of the General Secretary of Sport to declare the loss of office of every member of a sport institution because of the existence of an impediment or limitation foreseen in the Article 3 of the above law.

§2. National Olympic Committee and Sports Associations

I. Amateur Sport Organizations

A. *Introduction*

54. The National Olympic Committee, the national sport federations and unions and finally, the sport associations constitute the basic structural elements of the hierarchical pyramid of sport worldwide. In the following paragraphs, the basic kinds of sports institutions of amateur sports at the national level will be examined following the order of the law, from the bottom (associations, clubs) to the top.

B. *Sport Association*

1. The Notion of the Sport Association Within the Greek Legal System

55. Sport associations (amateur clubs) are the basic structural instruments of amateur sports in Greece.[1]

56. Article 1 of law 2725/1999 refers directly to the provisions of the CC for the associations (Articles 78, etc.), defining that the 'sport association is a union of people, according to the provisions of the Civil Code, whose main goal is the systematic cultivation and the development of the psychosomatic and intellectual capabilities of its athletes for their participation in sport events'.

1. Elements are taken from the work of A. Malatos, *Lessons of Sports Law*, 2005, 149, etc.

57. The Greek law accepts a priori the form of association as the only possible legal form of the first-degree amateur sport organizations. Even if it does not explicitly deny the foundation of other forms of sport organizations, with or without a legal personality, the provisions of law 2725/1999, especially Article 1 in combination with Article 8 (about the special athletic recognition), make it clear that it is not possible for a first-degree sport organization to function in a legal form other than the association, at least in the field of amateur sport. Besides, only associations may become members of unions or federations (Articles 10 and 19 of law 2725/1999).

58. Furthermore, the legal form of association is practically the most appropriate form for the achievement of the athletic goals since the people's union set out in Article 107 of the CC has no legal personality (so it cannot acquire any property, etc.) and the rest of the partnership forms involve a vivid financial and speculative goal, contrary to the idealistic and non-profit goal of the sport phenomenon as a kind of social activity. Even the civil company set out in Article 741 of the CC, although it has many features in common with the association, it does not provide the guarantees of the provisions regarding the associations (obligatory content of the statute, minimum number of members, etc.), to secure the achievement of the idealistic and non-profit goal of amateur sport.

59. The most basic provisions of the CC referring to the association are the following:

- Article 78, according to which a union of people pursuing a nonspeculative goal acquires a legal personality when it is registered in the special book held in the Court of its seat. There must be at least twenty persons for the foundation of an association.
- Article 79, according to which those who want to found an association have to submit a petition to the Court attaching the foundational act, the names of the members of the administration and the Constitution of the association, signed by at least twenty members.
- Article 80 refers to the minimum required content of the Constitution of the association.
- Articles 81–83 describe the procedure that follows the decision of the Court about the foundation of the association. According to Article 83, the association is considered existent when it is registered in the special book held in the Court of its seat.
- According to Article 84, every modification of the Constitution of the association has to be made with the same procedure as for its foundation.
- Article 85 refers to the disassembly of the association, defining that the disassembly has to be noted down in the same special book mentioned above.
- Articles 86–91 include provisions about the members of the association, their entrance, their exit, their expulsion, their rights and their obligations.
- Article 92 refers to the administration of the association, setting out that, unless there is no special provision in the Constitution of the association, the administration belongs to the members of the association.

- Articles 93–102 contain provisions about the supreme instrument of the association, which is the General Assembly. There are provisions about its summons, its competencies, the way it makes decisions, the conditions, the impediments and the procedure of elections, the nature of its decisions, etc. In particular, Article 101 defines that a decision of the General Assembly may be invalid if it is against the law or the Constitution of the association. This invalidity is declared by a civil court decision.
- Articles 103–106 refer to the disassembly of the association and its property after it, which, according to Article 106, may not be distributed to its members.

2. The Goal of the Sport Association

60. Article 1 of law 2725/1999 further defines the goal of the association as a sportive one since it sets out that 'the association has as its main goal the systematic cultivation and the development of the capabilities of its athletes for their participation in sport events'.

61. Sport events should be considered, according to the real meaning of the abovementioned legal provision, not any events, matches or games among individuals, but only those held in the framework of the official sport organizations of the specially recognized sport unions or federations. Consequently, the associations that are established with the aim to simply cultivate the physical education and the sportive development of their members, without having as the main goal the participation of their athletes in officially organized games and sport events, or the associations of which the athletes participate in unofficial sport organizations held by the associations themselves or by other unrecognized institutions, should not be considered sport associations under the real meaning of law 2725/1999.

62. The athletic goal of the association must be clearly stated within its statutes. Furthermore, Article 1 of law 2725/1999 demands that this goal is the main goal of the association. Associations established to serve mainly other goals (cultural, educational, etc.) without referring to sport as one of their main goals cannot be characterized as sport, nor can they be recognized as sport associations. However, sport is not necessarily the only main goal of a sport association. Sport Associations' statutes may contain various main goals, such as of cultural, educational, or recreational nature. Associations related to schools (i.e., graduate associations) or employees may also become sport associations by adding the goal of Article 1 of the law 2725/1999 in their statutes.

63. Finally, the Statutes of a sport association must define not only its goal but also the specific branches of sport activity the association intends to cultivate, as well as the procedure for the foundation of new branches of sport activity, according to Article 7, paragraph 8 of law 2725/1999.

3. The Non-profit Character of the Sport Association and Its Financial Function

64. The above-analysed goal of sport associations is pursued in the framework of their non-profit quality. The non-profit character of the sport associations is not directly defined in law 2725/1999, but it arises from the law's reference to the provisions of the CC about the associations. Article 78 of the CC sets out that 'the association should pursue a nonprofit goal'. This means that the associations must not pursue financial benefits that may result in the creation of wealth for them and profit for their members.

65. However, the nonspeculative character of the sport associations does not necessarily mean the abandonment of every financial function for the achievement of financial benefits. On the contrary, the acquisition of benefits is allowed when they result from the exploitation of its own property or from other activities, with the aim of securing the means of its survival and function since these benefits are not distributed to its members.

66. The financial function of sport associations is mainly regulated by Article 7 of law 2725/1999. Apart from the usual financial means (contributions of the members, subscriptions, gifts, allocations from the State, etc.), which must be set out in the statutes of the associations, there is a provision for the sport association that it can exercise a financial activity, in order to cover its functional needs, for example, it can offer lessons about the sports it cultivates to people other than its athletes, and it can prearrange fees for these lessons. According to the abovementioned provision, the financial activity of an association is only allowed when this activity intends to cover its functional needs, when it is limited to teaching the sports it cultivates and when these lessons are addressed to people other than the athletes of the association's competitive teams, in other words mainly to children.

67. In case the financial activity of the association does not meet the abovementioned conditions and terms, especially when this financial activity tends to serve the profit and not the coverage of the functional needs of the association, then, obviously, a matter of legal function of the association arises. This matter seems to be especially vivid to some associations, especially to those related to fighting sports, such as karate, judo, etc. These associations, under the coverage of the legal form of sport association, have as their main goal the teaching of their sports to others for money. This phenomenon also can be seen nowadays in other associations that are engaged with sports such as sailing, water skiing, etc., and even in associations with mass participation (football, basketball, etc.), which tend to create groups of educated athletes, the so-called academies, through which they offer for money lessons even to athletes for whom they have issued sports licences. This is why there is a serious discussion nowadays whether the abovementioned legal provision is compatible with the basic principle of associational law about the non-profit character of the sport associations or whether the same provision constitutes the means for the legalization of its violation.

68. The same discussion and the same problems arise with reference to the provision of Article 7, paragraph 4 of law 2725/1999, according to which, 'within the framework of the IOC regulations, the sport associations are allowed to sign contracts of sponsorship or advertising with individuals or legal entities'. According to the same legal provision, content of these contracts cannot be the grant of the use of the title or the emblem or other characteristic features of the association. However, even this prohibition seems to be infringed daily through the gradually increasing commercial exploitation of the emblems of the associations for speculative reasons.

69. Taking into consideration the abovementioned legal provisions, which legalize the already existent and always increasing financial activity of the sport associations, the provisions of paragraphs 3, 5, 9 and 10 of Article 7 seem to be of a limited practical meaning.

70. Paragraph 3 introduces the right of the sport associations to accept gifts from individuals or legal entities.

71. Paragraph 5 sets out the prohibition of the cohousing of sport associations and commercial companies, with the exception of the possibility of cohousing of sport associations with educational or labour organizations that founded these associations. This law provision aims to prevent associations from covering hidden commercial activity, but as mentioned above, without effectiveness. Commercial activities though related to catering and leisure within the sports facilities are included in a recent amendment of the respective Article 7 (law 5025/2023, Article 4) as an exception to the above prohibition.

72. Paragraph 9 sets out the prohibition of the partial or full sale or change of use of the sport facilities of the association. The sale or the change of use is only permitted after a decision of the General Assembly of the association, made with a majority of at least two-thirds of the association's members and followed by a judicial resolution, on condition that the needs of the association cannot be covered with other means or alternatives. The aim of this provision is the submission of the financial activity and the property of the association to the service of its athletic goal.

73. Paragraph 10 defines that in case of disassembly of the association, its fortune after the liquidation goes to the General Secretariat of Sports in favour of athletic goals. This provision constitutes a specialization of the general provision of Article 106 of the CC, which sets out that in case of disassembly of an association, its fortune is never distributed to its members.

4. Members of the Sport Association

74. Contrary to Article 78 of the CC, which does not clarify whether the members of the association can be individuals or legal entities, Article 1 of law 2725/1999 defines that members of a sport association can become only individuals. This limitation concerning the quality of the members of a sport association constitutes a basic feature of the first-degree sport organizations, which differentiates it from the second or third-degree organizations (unions, federations) since the last ones consist of legal entities and not of individuals.

75. Article 2, paragraph 1 sets out the minimum number of members of sport associations, which is the same set out in the general provision of Article 78 of the CC, i.e., twenty.

76. Article 2, paragraph 2 defines the details for joining a sport association as a member. If the candidate is proposed by two members, the Board of Administration of the association is obliged to decide on his/her entry within sixty days; otherwise, the candidate is considered to have already become a member of the association, and the President of the Board of Administration has to issue the relevant ascertaining act. If the Board of Administration rejects the candidate's application for entry with a fully explained decision or if the president does not issue the ascertaining act, the candidate may start an action to the regular court.

77. When the candidates are athletes of the association, who, according to Article 3, paragraph 5 of law 2725/1999, must have terminated their career at least a year ago and have achieved victories in Olympic, European, Mediterranean, Balkan or national events, the proposal of two members is not necessary for their entry. A simple application is enough.

78. The same legal provision sets out that an athlete of the association cannot become a member of it. This can only happen a year after his last participation in an official sport event, i.e., a sport event organized by the competent sport federation. The only exception to this rule is introduced in paragraph 6 of Article 3, according to which the athletes of shooting, golf, billiard, bowling, climbing, pancratium, horse riding, air sports, archery, waterskiing, tennis, squash, fencing, athletic fishing, triathlon, as well as from car and motor sports can be registered as members of their associations, if they are above 35 years old, while the athletes of chess, bridge and open sea sailing can be registered in their associations provided they are adults.

79. The reason for the prohibition of the athletes to be members of their associations seems to be the undistracted and unimpeded exercise of sport activity, free from administrative obligations. It is necessary though that the legislator reconsiders the above prohibition because the role of the athletes, especially the amateur ones, in their associations is today higher and more important. For this reason, the initial exception for very few sports has already been extended to much more, but the principle of the law that the role of the athlete is not compatible with the role of a member of an association remains the same.

80. Article 2, paragraph 1 of law 2725/1999 does not permit any discrimination among the members of a sport association, with the exception of the bestowment of the title of the 'honorary member' to those who have offered a great deal to the association or to sports in general. The only special treatment is set out in Article 2, paragraph 4 for the new members, who are entitled to vote and to be voted only a year after their entry into the association.

5. Limitations and Impediments for the Participation of Individuals in Sport Institutions (Associations, Unions, Federations)

81. In Article 3 of law 2725/1999, as modified several times (last with law 5025/2023), there is a list of impediments and limitations, the existence of which render the participation of individuals in a sport institution or in the administrative instruments of these institutions impossible.

82. According to Article 3, paragraph 1 of law 2725/1999, it is not allowed to participate as a member in the abovementioned sport institutions: (a) whoever has not completed his 18th year of age; (b) whoever has been referred to a hearing for a felony[2] or has been irrevocably convicted within the last decade for intentionally (and not by negligence) committing a crime belonging to a long list of the law, such as the crime of violence related with sports events, doping, homicide, espionage, robbery, stealing, larceny, bankruptcy, smuggling, tax evasion, bribery, forgery, scam, blackmail, crime against sexual freedom, breach of law for drugs and guns, etc., regardless of the sanction or to any misdemeanour with imprisonment of more than one year; (c) whoever has been peremptorily deprived of his political rights for as long as this deprivation lasts; and (d) whoever has been sentenced to deprivation of his sport quality according to Article 130, for as long as this deprivation lasts.

83. According to Article 3, paragraph 3 of law 2725/1999, in group sports, active referees and coaches cannot be members in associations engaged with the sport in which they activate. Exception has been recently included in the law for coaches who as athletes had achieved reaching a place between 1st and 8th in the Olympic Games, who may be simultaneously coaches and members of associations, unions or federations. Coaches are considered as active until two months after depositing their coaching licence in the respective federation. In case of breach of the above provisions, the participation of the active referee or coach in any association activity, including his/her election in any association organ, is invalid.[3]

84. According to Article 3, paragraph 4, active referees, judges, timekeepers and whoever takes part in a referee's activity of individual sports can be members of a sport association but cannot be members of its administration or representatives in

2. Long discussion has taken place recently regarding the prohibition of someone to participate as member in associations in case he has been referred to hearing for a felony, with the argument that this is against the presumption of innocence, but this provision remains unchanged.
3. The provisions of Art. 3, para. 1 of the law apply also according to para. 2 to the shareholders of AAEs with the exception of reference to a hearing for a felony, for which irrevocable conviction is required for the prohibition to be activated.

unions or federations. Exclusion for this provision stands for the referees, etc., of shooting, chess, bridge, air sports, archery, waterskiing, gymnastics and car and motor sports who can have full membership in associations, including the right to be elected in the Board or to represent them in unions and federations.

85. According to Article 3, paragraph 5 of law 2725/1999, athletes cannot become members of sport associations unless a year at least has passed since their participation in an official game, with the exception of sports referred to in paragraph 6, as already mentioned.

86. According to Article 3, paragraph 7, whoever has a work relation with the association, or provides it with his services or executes work for it, cannot become a member of it for at least one year after the end of this relationship.

87. Furthermore, Article 3, paragraph 7 of law 2725/1999 introduces a prohibition for merchants of car and motor parts to become members of the administration of car and motor sport associations.

88. According to Article 3, paragraph 8, absolute prohibition is provided for people who own, control or administer betting companies, their wives or husbands, as well as their second-degree relatives to become members of associations that cultivate sports, the games of which are accepted for bet.

89. If a person falling in one of the above limitations and impediments is already a member of an association or of its board of administration, he/she automatically loses this position, according to Article 3, paragraph 9. The Board of Administration is obliged to issue the ascertaining act for the deposition within fifteen days after it becomes aware of the impediment; otherwise, this act is issued by the General Secretary for Sport within the same deadline. With the same act, the General Secretary for Sport preaches to the Board members who failed to take the deposition decision within the above deadline of fifteen days as fallen from their position on the Board.

90. Finally, according to Article 4, paragraph 2 of law 2725/1999, the signing of any contract of a financial nature between the Board of Administration and a member of it or even a close relative of such a member constitutes a serious reason for the deposition of the Board of Administration itself. The difference though in this provision is that this deposition does not happen ex officio, but it must be announced with a judiciary resolution.

6. Board of Administration and General Assembly of the Sport Association

91. Sport associations are governed as foreseen in their statutes, which, having been controlled by a judge for their legality before their registration in the competent department of the Court, do not contain provisions against the law.

92. What constitutes a problem though in sport associations is that sports law lately contains unnecessary limitations and provisions which restrict the freedom of the sport associations without serious justification. For example, the law provides that the Board of Administration of a sport association may contain five to fifteen members. This provision, existing from the first version of law 2725/1999, could already be disputed as unjustified, although the law seems to provide only direction, leaving it to the discretion of its association to define the number of Board members. But lately, the fact that law amendments contain provisions, i.e., on how the voting will take place or when and how the list of members holding voting rights should be announced, goes far beyond the acceptable intervention of the state in the autonomy of sport.

93. The two main administrative organs of every association, as provided by law 2725/1999, are the Board of Administration (Article 4 of law 2725/1999) and the General Assembly (Article 5).

94. The Board of Administration, responsible for the administration of the association's activities, is composed as already mentioned of five up to fifteen members, as provided in the statutes, with a term of office of one up to three years, as provided also in the statutes. Some of them are appointed to the functions provided in the Statutes, such as the President, who is elected directly by the General Assembly, the Vice-president, General Secretary, Cashier, etc., who are elected by the Board in its first meeting.

95. All Board members must be members of the association with full voting rights. They are all volunteers and may not receive any fee for their participation in the association's activity. They may though receive amounts spent for transportation and accommodation whenever they travel for purposes related to the association. It is strictly prohibited for associations to sign any contract (labour, services, etc.) with Board members, their wives/husbands, children, parents, brothers or sisters, or even with legal entities to which any of the above persons participate. It is allowed though that a Board member makes cash facilities to the association to cover urgent needs.

96. Although it is clearly reasoned and justified, the law provision for the fully amateur character of the participation of one person to a sport association, during the last few years, the obligations and responsibilities of sports associations have increased so much that makes it very difficult for a nonprofessional to deal with them successfully, and this is the reason people are becoming reluctant in participating in sports associations. A possible solution to that should not necessarily be directed towards the change of character of this participation to professional. It could be enough to provide the obligation for every association to hire a manager who would deal with all the daily business of the association and would bear the responsibility in case of non-legality in its activities.

97. The General Assembly constitutes the highest authority within an association. It is composed of all members of the association and is competent for the most serious decisions, such as the amendment of the statutes, the election and control of the Board of Administration, the election of the control committee, the approval of the accounts, etc. Only members who have completed more than a year after their registration and have covered their subscription amount, as well as any other financial obligation towards the association, have the right to vote and be elected to the board or in any other position. The other members may attend the General Assembly and participate in the discussion but do not have the right to vote and be elected. The members' participation in the General Assembly is strictly personal, and no presence with a proxy or a representative is allowed by the law (Article 5, paragraph 2).

98. Article 5, as amended recently by law 4726/2020, contains provisions for the publication of the list of members with voting rights ten days before the General Assembly and the procedure for a member to react in case of disagreement.

99. It also contains unnecessary details for the voting for the election of board of administration. The election is made by an election committee composed of three members and elected by the general assembly, apart from its president who must be a lawyer member of the local Bar Association, which appoints him/her. The ballots contain different candidates for President and for Board members. The law also contains provisions on how many persons may vote every member, when someone is elected, and what happens in case of a tie, which used to be dealt with in the past by the associations themselves following the provisions of their statutes.

100. Needless to say, the COVID-19 experience led the law to provide the possibility of having the General Assembly organized via the internet with the use of technology in case it is required.

101. Apart from the above, all statutes provide the existence of a control committee elected by the General Assembly to control the financial administration of the association by the Board and report to the General Assembly, while only a few provide the existence of an EC or any similar organ composed by the President, the General Secretary, the Cashier and maybe some Board members with the task to deal with the everyday business of the association.

7. Special Athletic Recognition – Registry of Sports Associations

102. After the conclusion of the procedure for the judiciary recognition of the sport association, which is completed with its registration in the book of associations kept in the court of its seat, the association exists legally, but in order to be able to function within the framework of the provisions of law 2725/1999, it has to obtain the special recognition granted by the competent public instrument, which is, according to Article 8, paragraph 1, the competent organ of the Ministry of Sport or any other authorized organ of the central or regional administration.

103. The granting of the special athletic recognition is the necessary condition for the submission of the association to the provisions of law 2725/1999, with regard both to the control and supervisory competencies of the State on it and to privileges and the financial benefits a sport association can enjoy from the State. The special athletic recognition is the element that differentiates the sport associations from the regular associations of the CC.

104. Special athletic recognition is granted for every sport branch separately, and it does not necessarily concern all the sport activities of an association. If a sport association has more than one sports branch, it must obtain recognition for each one of them.

105. In the General Secretariat for Sports, there is a registry for the recognized sport associations functioning according to the provisions of Article 142 of law 4714/2020. The function of the Registry has been seriously criticized because of the bureaucratic character of the registration procedure and the number of documents required exceeding somehow the role of the state only to control the sport activity.

106. The special athletic recognition is granted under the following conditions:

- The sport association must be a member of a sport union or federation. All the above is proved with the certification of the competent union or federation. This condition has been legislated because the State wants to secure that the sport association really functions and cultivates the sport branch it has obtained the recognition for. If the sport association is occupied with a sport that does not belong to any officially recognized union or federation, it can obtain the special athletic recognition even without the certification of the union or the federation.
- The sport association must comply with all the general obligations set out for sport associations: (i) it must keep the books set out in Article 6 of law 2725/1999, (ii) it must submit its statute ratified by the court attached to along with a certification of registration in the same court, (iii) it must have a title in the Greek language, (iv) it must not use the title or trademark of any commercial company and enterprise. An exception to this last prohibition is set out for the sport associations founded by educational or working groups. These associations can bear the title of their founders.

107. As it has already been said, the sport association must neither be cohoused with a commercial company nor should its function hide the exercise of commercial activity; otherwise, its recognition is revoked, according to Article 8, paragraph 3 of law 2725/1999. Other cases of revocation of the special athletic recognition are when the associations do not employ a professional coach when it participates in events that are not approved by the respective federation or when it does not present the sport activity the statute its federation requires.

108. According to Article 8, paragraph 2, during the first two years from the registration of an association to a sports union or federation, the association may participate in any activity of the respective union or federation even without having received a special athletic recognition except for panhellenic competitions to which it may only participate if it possesses the special athletic recognition. If, after two years, the association has not received special athletic recognition and has not been registered in the Registry of Sports Associations, it loses the membership status of the respective union or federation and may no longer participate in its competitions except for the ones that have already started. The law also provides in Article 8, paragraph 4 prohibition for that association to use sports facilities that belong to persons controlled by the General Secretariat of Sport.

8. Merger of Sport Associations

109. Just like the former legal status did, law 2725/1999 emphasizes the perspective of the merger of the athletic associations so that larger sport units are created, and the division of the athletic social forces is prevented.

110. The merger of the sport associations is ruled today by the provisions of Article 9 of law 2725/1999 in combination with a ministerial decree containing its details and is allowed only for associations seated in the same region.

111. The merger can take place in two ways: either with the merger of two or more associations into one or, in team sports only, with the merger of parts of the same branch of sport of two or more associations. In this last case, the merged parts either create a new association or are merged through the absorption of one by the other, meaning that they continue to function as part of the absorbing association.

112. The association that results from the merger, as well as its new sport parts or the part of the absorbing association, takes part in the highest division of those the merged associations had the right to participate. The placing of the new association or part in this division is compulsory for the competent union or federation.

113. The association that results from the merger becomes de jure successor of the rights and obligations of the merged associations or parts.

C. Sport Union

1. Notion, Goal, Foundation and Function of the Sport Union

114. The sport associations, for each branch of sport they cultivate, may be unified, in regional level in regional unions. The provisions concerning the sport unions are found in Articles 10–17 of law 2725/1999. According to Article 10, sport unions have a legal personality as a body corporate of private law, established and functioning according to the provisions of Articles 78, etc., of the CC, i.e., in the legal form of association, which is the necessary form for the existence of the sport unions.

115. Although the sport unions function in the form of the association, there are many important differences between them and the sport associations, regarding their goals, their composition, and their function.

116. While the main goal of the sport association is the development of the capabilities of its athletes and the participation in sports events, the main goal of the sport union is to support the organization and develop the sport within the geographical framework of its competence and the organization of sports events, according to the regulations issued by the respective federations.

117. This geographical framework is, according to Article 11, paragraph 1 of law 2725/1999, the prefecture. Sport associations of which the seat is in the same prefecture can found a sport union, of which they become members, on condition that this union meets the special regulations and requirements of the relevant federation. This means that if the statute or the regulations of a federation do not allow the establishment and the function of sport unions, then although their foundation is possible according to the provisions of the CC, their existence has absolutely no importance for the athletic legal status. On the contrary, if the federation allows it, a sport union may include associations from different prefectures, especially in cases where some prefectures do not have the minimum number of associations required for the establishment of a sport union, i.e., ten, according to Article 10, paragraph 1 of law 2725/1999.

118. According to Article 17, paragraph 1, a sport union also needs the special athletic recognition, just like the sport associations. For this recognition, it is necessary that the respective sport federation expresses its positive and fully explained opinion. The same happens in case of revocation of the special athletic recognition, which can happen after a fully explained opinion of the relevant federation or in case the sport union breaches the law, according to Article 17, paragraph 2 of law 2725/1999 (is cohoused with a commercial business or has hidden commercial activity or does not show sports activity as mentioned in its statutes and in the statutes of the respective federations or does not keep the books as required by the law).

119. Members of the sport union can become the sport associations on condition that they meet the requirements set out in the statute and the regulations of the federations. The minimum number of associations required by the law to be members of a union to be created or continue its activity is ten. A union may be established by a decision of its founding General Assembly after a decision of the Board of Administration of the associations that have decided to establish it. The entry of an association into a sport union is made according to Article 11, paragraph 3 of law 2725/1999. For the entry, there must be a decision of the Board of Administration of the sport union. For the elimination of the association from a sport union, there must be a decision from the General Assembly of the union.

120. The supreme organ of a sports union as well as of any association is the General Assembly which functions as provided in Article 14 of law 2725/1999 as amended by laws 4726/2020 and 4908/2022. With the above amendments, the legislator tried to stop the arbitrariness in the function of sports unions and federations and to establish stricter control of the state, limiting though impermissibly the autonomy of the sports organizations.

121. The General Assembly of a sports union is composed of representatives of its member associations who are appointed by the decision of their Boards of Administration. As provided in the recent law amendments, the representatives must necessarily be Board members. This amendment aims to stop the phenomenon of associations being represented by persons not really connected to them in agreement with candidates or members of the union or federation they intend to support, especially in electoral procedures. This phenomenon was quite often in the past in federations, but much less in the unions, because their local character makes it difficult for someone not really connected with an association to represent it in the General Assembly of a sports union. For this reason, this recent amendment of the law even if it is quite justified for the federations is too strict for the unions.

122. Each association representative may only represent one association, and every association member has one vote in the General Assembly of the Union it participates.

123. The law provides in paragraph 2 of Article 14 restrictions on the voting rights of associations in the union's General Assembly. In order to obtain full voting rights and the right to propose candidates for election in the organs of the union, an association must: (i) have special athletic recognition, (ii) be registered in the Registry of Sports Associations, and have participated during two of the last previous years without taking into consideration the year of the General Assembly, if it takes place before 30 June, participated in official competitions with at least eight athletes and for team sports twelve athletes per year. The statutes of the sports associations may include additional limitations, such as the obligation of the association to cover any debt towards the union.

124. The law also provides some requirements for the preparation of the General Assembly and the election of the Board of Administration of sports unions. The invitation must be announced forty-five days before the day of the General Assembly (twenty-five days if it is extraordinary), and the unions must send a list of the associations with voting rights in the General Assembly to the General Secretariat of Sport to confirm that they fulfil the first two criteria mentioned above (special athletic recognition and registration in the Registry).

125. Although members of the sport unions can become only the sport associations, represented in the General Assembly by an authorized member of their Board of Administration, members of the sport union's Board of Administration can only become individuals, members – not necessarily of their Board – of the participating sport associations with the right to vote and to be elected in the association's organs and proposed by them to the sport union's General Assembly. Those individuals are consequently governed by the limitations and impediments that also rule their participation in the sport associations and the administration of them, according to Article 12. Furthermore, according to Article 12, paragraphs 2, 3 and 4, the individuals may not be candidates to be elected as members of the instruments of a sport union if they are Board members of another sports union when submitting their candidacy or employees of another sport union or federation until one and two months respectively prior to submitting the candidacy or of the General Secretariat of Sports.

126. In case a member of the administration of a sport union is later elected as a member of the administration of another sport union or federation, he is considered to have de jure resigned from his previous position, according to Article 13, paragraph 3 of law 2725/1999.

127. The number of members of the Board of Administration of each sport union depends on the number of the associations – members of the union, according to Article 13, paragraph 1, and it may vary from seven to fifteen members. The election of Board members takes place every four years in the General Assembly by the electoral committee, the President of which should be a lawyer appointed from the local Bar Association. As foreseen for the associations, the President is elected directly from the General Assembly with a separate vote for candidates to this position from candidates to become Board members.

128. During its first meeting, the newly elected Board appoints among its members the Vice-President, the General Secretary, the Cashier and any other position provided in the statutes of the union. According to Article 12, paragraph 4 of the law, members holding such positions should have their domicile in the geographical area of the union.

129. The sport union functions subject to the regulations of the relevant federation, to the provisions of the CC and law 2725/1999, according to Articles 15 and 16 of this law. Some of the law provisions for the associations, like the books they are obliged to keep, their right to accept donations, to sign sponsorship agreements and the prohibition to be cohoused with a commercial business, also apply to sports unions.

130. In case a sport union ceases its function, its property goes to the relevant sport federation and not to the General Secretariat of Sports, as it happens with the sport associations.

2. Local Committee

131. In case the existing sport associations in a prefecture or in a region are less than ten and because of the geographical particularities, the foundation of a sport union together with the sport associations of the neighbouring regions is not possible, a local committee can be founded by decision of the relevant sport federation.

132. The function of the local committee set out in Article 18 of law 2725/1999, is completely different. While the sport unions can function either as members of the federation or as its simple administrative branches, the local committees can only work as administrative branches of the federation. The local committees do not possess any legal personality, and therefore, they are not subject to the procedure of the special athletic recognition. Their function is ruled by the provisions of a special regulation, which the federation has to issue so that the local committees can legally work within its gulfs.

3. Sport Federation

133. The system of organization of sport associations in sport federations may follow two main models of organization. The sport associations can either directly be organized as members of second-degree institutions, the national sport federations, or they can be unified at the beginning in local sport unions, which are then unified in a third-degree institution, the national sport federation.

134. Nowadays, the only sport in which members of the relevant sport federations are not the sport associations themselves but the local sport unions is football. This is easily understandable by the great number of football sport associations, a fact that allows the creation of a sport union in each prefecture of the country.

135. In the other sports, due to the small number of sport associations, members of the relevant federations are the associations themselves and not the sport unions. This does not exclude the creation of local unions or committees, which either hold local sport events or simply constitute administrative branches of the federation for the service of the sport within the borders of their territorial competence. But in this case, the local unions or the committees are not members of the federation, although they may possess a legal personality. According to Article 19 of law 2725/1999, the sport associations or the regional sport unions that cultivate the same branch of sport can found sport federations, i.e., second-degree or third-degree sport institutions, which cultivate this sport and take care of its development at a national level.

136. Members of the sport federations are the founding sport associations or the founding regional sport unions as well as the sport associations and the sport unions that may join the sport federation after its foundation. According to Article 19, paragraph 1, the sport federation of each sport or branch of sport is the supreme athletic institution on a national level and is also established according to the provisions for the associations set out in the CC.

137. According to the second paragraph of the same article, the sport federation is recognized to have a monopolistic place since only one federation is allowed to be established for each sport or branch of sport. This federation represents the sport internationally, according to the regulations of the relevant sport federation and the International Olympic Committee (IOC).

138. The function of the sport federation is ruled by the general provisions of the CC and the special provisions of law 2725/1999. For its foundation, at least twenty sport associations or five sport unions that cultivate the same branch of sport are required. Regarding the membership, the registration of associations or unions as members, their representation in the general assembly, the limitations on the voting right, the elections as well as the limitations and impediments for the participation of individuals in sport institutions as per Article 3 of the law apply as in the sports unions (*see* above)

139. The number of members of the Board of Administration of each sport federation depends on the number of the associations – members of the federation, according to Article 22, paragraph 1, and it may vary from five to twenty-one members. They are elected for four-year term by the General Assembly which should take place during the last four months of the year of the Olympic Games, except for the HFF (Greek Football Federation (EPO)) which elects its Board during the months of June and July of the year of the Olympic Games and at least thirty days prior to the beginning of the following season.

140. The recent law amendments (law 4809/2021) have inserted two revolutionary changes in the function of sports federations.

141. In Article 22 of law 2725/1999, paragraph 6 now provides that in the Board meetings of the sports federations participate one representative of the active athletes and one representative of the active coaches appointed by the respective association of athletes or coaches and in case of nonexistence by decision of the Board of the federation. The representatives of athletes and coaches may not be elected Vice-Presidents or General Secretaries or Cashiers of the federations. The same article also provides for the participation of a representative of referees in the Board meetings of EPO without voting rights. This revolutionary amendment covers a need raised seriously in the past that the federations while being the supreme authority of every sport, were functioning without even taking into account the opinion of those who are the protagonists of sports, the athletes, as well as the coaches and the referees.

142. Paragraph 7 of the same Article 22 introduces for the first time additional limitations to the Board members and especially the persons who hold the office of President, Vice-President, General Secretary and Cashier of a federation. According to these: (i) a President may only serve three full or partial terms of office, (ii) a Vice-President, General Secretary and Cashier may only serve one of these offices two consecutive full or partial terms and may not be reelected before two years lapse from the last term of office, and (iii) any person above 70 years old may not be elected as Board member, while he may be appointed in any non-elected position.

143. The way of election of the members of the Board of Administration is set out in Article 24, according to which the respective provisions of Article 14 for the membership, the representation, the right to vote (with a small differentiation as per paragraph 2), the preparation of the General Assembly and the elections in sports unions apply to the federations as well. The elections may take place in the seat of every union simultaneously upon the decision of the General Assembly of the Federation as provided in the amended paragraph 3 of Article 24. The General Assembly of the federations is the competent organ to elect according to the provisions of their statutes their representatives in the HOC.

144. The HFF has always been excluded from the above principles (Article 24 paragraph 6 of the law 2725/1999) since, for years in the General Assembly, only unions had the right to participate with one representative each. The major scandals of corruption and match-fixing which caused the intervention of Federation International des Football Associations (FIFA) and Union of European Football Associations (UEFA) recently,[4] caused a series of major changes both in statutory and organizational matters. The statutes of the HFF have changed several times over the past few years, and after a period when each union had three votes, while clubs of the top division (Super League) obtained the right to vote represented by one person each, today it contains a modern approach which could be used as a model for other federations in the future.[5] Today, the current statutes contain the provision that the General Assembly is composed as follows: (a) fifty-three representatives of the fifty-three sports unions of the country (one per each), (b) sixteen representatives for the Super League Greece, which is a member of EPO (one per participating club in the top division), (c) one representative from each of the following unions: Football League (second division clubs), Women's Football, Beach Soccer, Futsal, Player's, Coaches' and Referees' Unions.

145. The law includes provisions for the employees of the federations (Article 30), the right to hire a general manager (called by law special associate – Article 23), and the obligation to hire a consultant in sports psychology (Article 23A – new).

146. The sport federation keeps records of athletes and coaches (Article 26, paragraph 2) and issues special regulations, which rule the organization and the operation of the sport and are obligatory for its member associations (Article 27). The following regulations are obligatory: (i) competitions regulations, (ii) national teams regulations, (iii) athletes registration and transfer regulations, (iv) disciplinary regulations, (v) deontology regulations, (vi) anti-doping regulations, and (vii) refereeing regulations For the institution of these regulations, the internationally

4. According to Art. 5 of the law 4431/2016, which intended to cover exactly this intervention and the nomination of a temporary Board appointed by FIFA for a short period of less than a year in order to reorganize the HFF, it is acceptable in any sport to be appointed by the respective international federation special administrative organs for a limited period in order to face urgent and special situations. The above organs replace for this period the statutory organs of the national federation.
5. One of the main disadvantages of the current system in sports federations is that only associations are represented in their General Assembly, while athletes, coaches, referees and other participants may not participate unless invited and in any case without vote.

valid regulations must be taken into account. At the same time, the State is competent to control the legality of these regulations so that it can secure their compatibility with both the Greek legislation and the relevant international federation's regulations. Article 66, paragraph 3 of the law 4410/2016, which was introduced after the scandals in the Hellenic football, added paragraph 7 in Article 26, according to which it is obligatory for all national federations to adopt Deontology Codes and establish Deontology Committees harmonized with the similar codes and procedures of the respective international federations or the IOC. It is also obliged to incorporate in its regulations the regulations of the IOC about doping (Article 26, paragraph 4)

147. Similar obligations of the federations regarding the control and the supervision of their national duties and relations are set out in Article 26, paragraphs 3 and 6.

148. The same supervisory and control function from the part of the State also institutes Article 28, which sets out the procedure for the giving of the special athletic recognition to the sport federations. The special athletic recognition is not compulsory for the State unless there is a separate international sport federation recognized by the IOC (Article 28 paragraph 1). Special procedures and conditions for the athletic recognition are set out in Article 28, paragraph 3 for the federations that are separated from already existent sport federations. Finally, according to Article 28, paragraphs 2 and 4, the special athletic recognition is revoked either owing to general reasons with a decision of the Deputy Minister of Sports or because of the fact that the number of the legally activated associations of the federations has declined to fifteen.

149. The legal consequences of the special athletic recognition to the sport federations are similar to those for the sport associations and the sport unions. But the most important consequence of the athletic recognition is the fact that the federation is recognized as the only official sport authority at a national level, with official organizing, administrative and disciplinary powers for its sport, which the State is obliged to control on the basis of the special provisions of Article 51 (about the managing obligations of the federations), Article 52 (about the surveillance and control by the General Inspector of Public Administration) and Article 52A (about the onsite control of sports institutions by small groups of employees of the General Secretariat of Sport) and to allocate according to the procedure set out in Article 50 of law 2725/1999.

150. The legal nature of the sport federation in Greece has a lot in common with the legal nature of the respective federations throughout Europe. The sport federations in Greece are not instruments of the National Olympic Committee, despite the fact that delegates from each sport federation take part in the Plenary Session of the National Olympic Committee.

151. Both the monopolistic position of the federation as well as its competencies are secured with Articles 19, 27 and 119 of law 2725/1999.

152. The most important difference regarding the legal nature of the Greek federations compared to the federations of other European countries has to do with the more intense control the State exercises on them.[6] The Greek federations are subject to rules concerning the Constitution and the election of their administrations, the function of their general assemblies, the books they are obliged to keep, the control of the legitimacy of their regulations and decisions, the approval of their financial activities, the employment of foreign coaches, the definition of the conditions for the transfers of athletes, the definition of the national divisions and the number of teams for each division, the exercise of the disciplinary power, the settlement of the financial disputes, etc. Especially in team sports, the abovementioned rules are rather detailed. It seems absolutely necessary that the control of the State remains limited to issues related to the public order, the investigation of penal crimes and the proper use of any income coming from public authorities. This would enable not only the autonomous growth of sports but also their rapid development and adaptation to the new era and better funding. On the contrary, the obligation for the education of the Board members and the employees of all sports federations (as well as associations and unions), which seems a necessity but is not yet foreseen in the law, would definitely assist the same goal.

153. The Olympic Greek sport federations are the following:

- The League of the Hellenic Gymnastic and Sport Associations (SEGAS) (www.segas.gr).
- The HFF (EPO) (www.epo.gr).
- The Hellenic Basketball Federation (EOK) (www.basket.gr).
- The Hellenic Volleyball Federation (EOPE) (www.volleyball.gr).
- The Hellenic Swimming Federation (KOE) (www.koe.org.gr).
- The Hellenic Handball Federation (OHE) (www.handball.org.gr).
- The Hellenic Federation of Weightlifting (EOAV) (www.weightlifting.gr).
- The Hellenic Federation of Wrestling (EOFP) (www.elop.gr).
- The Hellenic Sailing Federation (EIO) (www.eio.gr).
- The Hellenic Gymnastic Federation (EGO) (www.ego-gymnastics.gr).
- The Hellenic Boxing Federation (EOP) (www.hellenicboxing.org.gr).
- The Hellenic Cycling Federation (EOP) (https://hellenic-cycling.gr).
- The Hellenic Sport Federation of Table Tennis (EFOEPA) (www.httf.gr).
- The Hellenic Sport Federation of Tennis (EFOA) (www.efoa.gr).
- The Hellenic Rowing Federation (EKOFNS) (www.kopilasia.gr).
- The Hellenic Canoe Kayak Federation (EO CANOE KAYAK) (www.canoekayak.gr).
- The Hellenic Shooting Federation (SKOE) (www.skoe.gr).
- The Hellenic Sport Federation of Archery (EFOT) (www.archery.org.gr).

6. In practice, although the external control especially in financial issues by the State and other competent authorities has become more intense lately, it is still considered ineffective. The obligation to follow in parallel real internal control procedures in the sport federations already foreseen by their statutes could be proven even more effective. On the contrary the law as amended after the financial crisis treats the sport federations as public authorities, while by legal nature they should be considered as private ones and does not enable them to find new ways of funding.

– The Hellenic Fencing Federation (EOX) (www.fencing.org.gr).
– The Hellenic Equestrian Federation (EOI) (www.hef.gr).
– The Hellenic Judo Federation (EOT) (www.hjf.gr).
– The Hellenic Tae Kwon Do Federation (ELOT) (www.elot-tkd.gr).
– The Hellenic Badminton Federation (EOFSA) (www.badminton.gr).
– The Hellenic Modern Pentathlon Federation (EOMP)[7] (www.eomop.gr).
– The Hellenic Hockey Federation (www.hellenichockey.gr).
– The Hellenic Skate Federation (https://skatehellas.gr).
– The Hellenic Baseball Softball Federation (https://greeksoftball.gr).
– The Hellenic Karate Federation (EΛOK) (www.elok.gr).
– The Hellenic Federation of Mountaineering & Climbing (EOOA) (www.eoo-a.gr).
– The Hellenic Golf Federation (www.hgf.gr).
– The Hellenic Winter Sports Federation (EOHA) (https://wintersports.gr/).

4. The Hellenic Olympic Committee

154. The sports organization was founded on 24 November 1894 under the name 'Olympic Games Committee' (EOA) for the purpose of organizing the first modern Olympic Games and which acquired legal status as a public legal entity with Article 35 of the BCCA law of 10 July 1899, was reorganized by Law 3148/1955 and renamed as 'Hellenic Olympic Committee' (E.O.E. and in English H.O.C. – www.hoc.gr) by paragraph 1 of Article 37 of Law 2725/1999 and the PD 130/2000 which contained its statutes, is transformed by law 4639/2019, already amended once by law 4957/2022, into a non-profit legal entity under private law, fully self -governing and supervised by the Ministry of Sports.

155. The statute of E.O.E. and its amendments are voted by its Plenary Session, with a decision taken by a quorum of at least two-thirds of the members and a majority of at least two-thirds of the valid votes, approved by the IOC and are included in laws 4639/2019 and 4957/2022.

156. The purpose of the E.O.E. is the development, promotion and protection of the Olympic Movement in Greece, according to the Olympic Charter. The purpose and responsibilities of the E.O.E. include in particular:

(a) The care for the correct interpretation and application of the fundamental principles, values and rules of the Olympic Charter and the supervision and assurance of its observance in Greece.
(b) The promotion of the fundamental principles and values of Olympism in Greece, especially in the fields of sports and education. For this purpose, the EO: (aa) ensures the dissemination of Olympic education, (bb) promotes the integration of Olympic educational programs at all school levels and in higher

7. Triathlon has been recently included in the competence of EOMP.

education institutions, (cc) supports, with every way and means, the operation of the National Olympic Academy, (dd) encourages the establishment of Olympic Museums and Institutes of all kinds dedicated to Olympic Education, as well as the development of sports, cultural and other actions or programs related to the Olympic Movement.

(c) The dissemination and defence of the principles of sportsmanship in accordance with the Code of Ethics of the I.O.C.

(d) The propagation among the youth of the love of sports and respect for the sports and Olympic ideal.

(e) The encouragement, supervision and financial support of high-performance sport, as well as sport for all.

(f) The organization and implementation of training programs for sports administrators and any other type of seminars or events that promote the principles and values of Olympism.

(g) The implementation of the actions and interventions approved by its Plenary Session, following the recommendation of its regular committees, as well as the contribution, in any way and means, to the actions of the International and National Olympic Academy or other bodies with the task of spreading of the Olympic principles and values, according to the Olympic Charter of the IOC.

(h) The development and implementation of actions and interventions against all forms of discrimination and violence in sports, as well as the development and implementation of actions to raise awareness and inform society about the fight against all forms of discrimination and violence in sports.

(i) The monitoring of the implementation of the World Anti-Doping Code (World Anti-Doping Code) by the sports bodies concerned, as well as the adoption and implementation of rules and policies to combat and prevent doping in accordance with the rules and principles of the World Anti-Doping Code and the role and tasks that this Code assigns to National Olympic Committees, in particular regarding the requirements for participation in competitions or financial support of athletes and the relevant federations and in general the management of the results of anti-doping controls.

(j) The monitoring of the implementation of the Code of the I.O.C. to prevent match manipulation and to inform athletes and sports Federations about its provisions.

(k) The encouragement and support of measures for medical treatment and in general the assurance and promotion of the health of athletes.

(l) The financial grant and the general support, by any other means or way, of the national sports federations of its members for the development, dissemination and promotion of the Olympic sports and for the preparation of the athletes who will represent Greece in the summer or winter Olympic Games, the European Games, the Mediterranean Games, the Youth Olympic Games and any other continental or intercontinental games held under the auspices of the IOC, the European Olympic Committees or the International Union of Mediterranean Games, as well as the direct financial support of athletes for their preparation and participation in the above competitions, after the consent of the sports federation to which they belong.

(m) The general administration and management of all kinds of sports and non-sports facilities that belong to it by ownership or have been granted to it for use, the annexes and the surrounding areas, in particular the Kallimarmaro Panathenaic Stadium, the Olympic Swimming Pool of Athens, the facility of Ancient Olympia and the Museum of Modern Olympic Games, etc. Within these frameworks, the E.O.E. grants the use of its stadiums and other facilities to third parties for the organization of matches, conferences, cultural, social and any other kind of events, against consideration.
(n) The protection by any legal and appropriate means, including recourse to justice, of the real rights over its properties.
(o) The participation of its representatives in the administration of the Olympic Sports Center of Athens (O.A.K.A.) in accordance with the applicable provisions.
(p) The issue and distribution of commemorative coins, medals, stamps and other items on the occasion of the summer and winter Olympic Games, the European Games, the Mediterranean Games, the Youth Olympic Games and any other continental or intercontinental competition under the auspices of the IOC, the European Olympic Committees or the International Union of Mediterranean Games.
(q) The publication and distribution of albums, special editions regarding the development and promotion of the Olympic Idea, the history of Olympism and sports in general, informational material and all kinds of publications.
(r) The granting of licences to use its emblems.
(s) The conclusion of sponsorship contracts with third parties (sponsors).
(t) Any other authority assigned to it by law, as well as any authority assigned to the National Olympic Committees by the Olympic Charter.

157. In the exclusive competence of the E.O.E. belongs:

(a) The final selection of athletes representing Greece each time at the Summer or Winter Olympic Games, the European Games, the Mediterranean Games, the Youth Olympic Games and any other continental or intercontinental games held under the auspices of the IOC, the European Olympic Committees or the International Union of Mediterranean Games.
(b) The choice of the city, which can claim to host in Greece, summer or winter Olympic Games, Youth Olympic Games, European Games organized by the Union of European Olympic Committees, Mediterranean Games or other continental or intercontinental games that are under the auspices of the IOC, the European Olympic Committees or the International Union of Mediterranean Games, as well as the supervision of the organization of the above games unless otherwise specified in the Olympic Charter.
(c) The care for the ceremony of the Touching of the Olympic Flame in Ancient Olympia and the ceremony of its Delivery, as well as for the conduct of the Olympic Torch Relay in the Greek Territory for the summer and winter Olympic Games and for any other case decided by the Plenary of, in collaboration with the IOC.

(d) The granting of licences to use the symbol of the host city of the Olympic Games after approval by the IOC.
(e) The issuance of interpretative circulars with the aim of removing any doubt or dispute regarding the interpretation and application of the provisions herein, the internal regulations and decisions of the Greek Olympic Committee (EOE), the provisions of the Olympic Charter, the regulations and the decisions of the D.O.E. or regarding the rights, duties and obligations of each of them or regarding any other matter arising from the operation of the E.O.E.

158. To achieve its goals, E.O.E. can:

(a) undertake the implementation of EU programs or participate in them in cooperation with other National Olympic Committees or with other international or non-international sports organizations;
(b) enter into collaborations with non-governmental or governmental organizations, provided that the object, terms and general context of such collaborations are in accordance with the principles and rules of the Olympic Charter; and
(c) recommend to the Minister of Sports or any other competent Minister the adoption of legislative and administrative measures that contribute to the realization of its purposes.

159. For the optimal management and utilization of its property and the fulfilment of its purposes, E.O.E. may establish non-profit legal entities.

160. E.O.E. enjoys operational independence and maintains full autonomy and autonomy in the administration and management of its affairs in general. It is supervised by the Minister of Sports, in accordance with paragraph 9 of Article 16 of the Constitution, only with regard to the management of the regular or extraordinary state grants it receives.

161. The resources of E.O.E. are:

(a) The regular annual and any extraordinary special purpose state grant of paragraph 2 of Article 5.
(b) The sums it collects from the IOC, the Union of European Olympic Committees, the International Union of Mediterranean Games, the other National Olympic Committees, the International Sports Federations and other International Sports Organizations in the fulfilment of its statutory purposes.
(c) The income from Olympic Games, Mediterranean Games, Youth Olympic Games, European Games and European Youth Olympic Festivals held in Greece or abroad, pursuant to an agreement with the respective organizing body.
(d) The revenues from the granting of licences for the use of its emblems as well as the revenues from the granting of licences for the use of the symbol of the host city of the Olympic Games.
(e) Grants from legal entities of public or private law, inheritances, bequests, donations from members or third parties and all kinds of contributions and benefits in money and in kind in favour of it.

(f) The income in general from its movable and immovable property, in particular from the exploitation of the facilities it administers or manages.
(g) The income from the organization of sports competitions, cultural, social and any other kind of events.
(h) The revenues from granting the use of the stadiums and other facilities to third parties for the organization of competitions, conferences, cultural, social and any other kind of events.
(i) The income from the exploitation of the advertising spaces of its sports facilities, in accordance with Article 56 of law 2725/1999 (A' 121).
(j) The income from the issuance and distribution of the special souvenirs and the editions.
(k) The income from the sponsorship contracts.
(l) Any other income with legal origin.

162. The members of E.O.E. are divided into voting members and non-voting members. Only the members with the right to vote and, in the case of sports federations, their representatives have the right to be elected to the Presidium of the Plenary Session of the E.O.E. (i.e., in the positions of President, First and Second Vice-President, General Secretary and Treasurer) and the EC.

163. Members of the E.O.E., with the right to one vote each, are:

(a) In their capacity (ex officio) and for as long as they maintain this capacity, the members of IOC for Greece, if and as long as they exist.
(b) The national sports federations that cultivate sports that are included in the official program of the upcoming summer and winter Olympic Games (Olympic sports), as long as they cumulatively meet the following conditions: (aa) have a special sports recognition from the General Secretariat of Sports (G.G.A.) in accordance with the current legislation, (bb) are recognized members of the respective international sports federation, and (cc) meet the conditions defined by the Olympic Charter. Every sports federation that meets the above conditions participates in the Plenary Session of the E.O.E. with one representative and has the right to one vote, even if he cultivates more than one Olympic sport. The representative of each federation is elected, together with his deputy, by the General Assembly (GA) of the federation no later than 31 December of the year immediately preceding the year in which the Electoral Plenary Session meets.
(c) An athlete who has participated in a summer or winter Olympic Games, who is elected, together with his alternate, by the Association of Participants in Olympic Games (E.S.O.A.).
(d) Two athletes, one male and one female, together with their alternates, who are elected by the members of the last delegation of the Summer Olympic Games as members of the Athletes' Committee of the EOE. and representatives of this Committee in the Plenary Session of the E.O.E.
(e) Two personalities of recognized prestige, one man and one woman, with a contribution to sports and the dissemination of the Olympic spirit, who are elected by the Plenary session.

164. The position of the representative of a national sports federation member of the E.O.E. in the Plenary Session of the E.O.E., as well as the position of the elected member of the E.O.E., is honorary and unpaid.

165. Members of the E.O.E. without the right to vote are the national sports federations that cultivate Olympic sports and do not meet the above conditions as long as they have not been included in another federation with special sports recognition by the decision of the Minister responsible for sports. Each such federation is represented in the Plenary Session of the E.O.E. with a representative, who is elected, together with his deputy, by the General Assembly. of the federation.

166. The members of the IOC for Greece are permanent members of the EOE. The representatives of the national sports federations and the elected members, as well as their substitutes, are elected for a four-year term, which begins on 1 January of the following year from their election and ends on 31 December of the year of the next Summer Olympic Games. The representatives of the national sports federations – members of the E.O.E., as well as the elected members are eligible for re-election.

167. It is not allowed to be elected as representative of a sports federation or a member of E.O.E. persons who (a) have not completed the 21st year of age at the time of election, (b) are under deprivation or subsidiary judicial support, full or partial, (c) fall under the limitations of Article 3 of Law 2725/1999, (d) have been punished by the IOC, for any reason and to any penalty, in accordance with the Olympic Charter, and (e) have been punished by the Ethics and Ethics Fan Character Committee.

168. It is not allowed to be elected representatives of a sports federation (a) those who run an individual business with the object of producing or trading sports clothing, footwear, sports equipment and any other kind of sports goods, as well as those who have the status of a full or limited member of a company with the same object as above, (b) those who maintain a betting agency and their spouses. Excluded are Olympians who received a prediction agency licence in accordance with Law 2166/1993, (c) the shareholders of the joint-stock company with the name 'Football Predictions Organization S.A.' (O.P.A.P. S.A.) or of a company that is allowed to provide betting games with predetermined returns according to Articles 45 to 50 of Law 4002/2011 and their spouses, (d) employees, permanent or under contract of private law: (aa) of the General Secretariat of Sports and the bodies supervised by it, (bb) of the national sports federations that are members of the E.O.E., with or without the right to vote, and (cc) any other State body, legal entity under public law or organization, body or service of Local Self-Administration Organizations (OTA), with the subject of sports. Olympians who have been appointed or seconded to such positions in accordance with current legislation are excluded.

169. Organs of E.O.E. are: (1) The Plenary Session and (2) The EC. The members of the E.O.E. convene in a meeting during the period from 15 to 31 January of the year following the summer Olympic Games (Electoral Plenary Session) in order to elect: (a) the President, the First and Second Vice-Presidents, the General Secretary and his deputy, the Treasurer and his deputy, and (b) the President of the International

Olympic Academy (IOC), the President of the National Olympic Academy (IOC), the President of the Olympic Preparation Committee (IOC.), the President of the Olympic Torch Relay Committee (O.P.O.L.) and the President of the Sports Spirit, Ethics and Ethics Committee, after his deputy. Within fifteen days from the meeting of the Electoral Plenary Session, the President of the E.O.E. reconvenes the Plenary Session in order to elect: (a) the persons of recognized authority, (b) the other members of the International Olympic Academy., except for the President and the General Secretary of the E.O.E. and the members of the IOC. for Greece (if any), which are ex officio members of International Olympic Academy, (c) the other members of the Board of Directors of the National Olympic Academy, (d) the other members of the Committees, and (e) the Deans of the establishments.

170. The Plenary Session is the supreme body of the E.O.E. and decides on every issue related to the purpose and responsibilities of the E.O.E., which does not fall under the exclusive competence of another body. The Plenary session is only competent to decide on: (a) any amendment to the statutes of the E.O.E., (b) the election of the persons referred to in Articles 12 and 13, (c) the approval of the report, budget of the E.O.E. and annual financial statements and reports, (d) the approval of the operating regulations of the Regular Committees of the EOE, (e) the formation of Special Committees and the regulation of every issue related to their operation, including the approval of their operating regulations, (f) issuing interpretive circulars regarding the interpretation and application of its statutes and internal regulations, (g) any other matter that is expressly defined in the law or in this statute as falling under its exclusive competence. The Plenary Session consists of the members of the D.O.E. for Greece, the representatives of its member sports Federations and the elected members of Article 7. It meets regularly once every month and exceptionally whenever there is a need or if this is requested in writing by one-third of the total number of its members with the right to vote for the discussion of a special and specific issue, which is specialized in the relevant application.

171. The EC is competent to: (a) exercise the administration and management of the daily affairs of the E.O.E., (b) decide on every matter that pertains to the responsibilities of the E.O.E. after a relevant authorization by the Plenary, (c) submit a proposal to the Plenary regarding the approval of the report and the budget of the E.O.E., as well as regarding the annual financial statements and reports, (d) recommend to the Plenary the formation and operation of Special Committees and to take charge of the recommendations of these Committees, (e) oversee the drafting of the operating regulations of the offices, sports or non-sports facilities and regular Committees of the EOE and to coordinate them, (f) approve the expenses related to the current operation, the facilities and the construction of projects of the E.O.E. and to conduct public tenders, up to the amount determined each time by the Plenary.

172. The EC of the E.O.E. consists of: (a) the President, (b) the members of the D.O.E. for Greece, if any, which are defined ex officio members of the EU, (c) the First Vice-President, (d) the Secretary-General, (e) the Treasurer, and (f) the President of the Athletes' Committee.

173. In E.O.E., the following regular Committees operate:

(a) the Olympic Preparation Committee;
(b) the Olympic Torch Relay Committee;
(c) the Philatelic Sports Spirit, Ethics and Deontology Committee (EFIPID);
(d) the Athletes' Committee;
(e) the Committee for Gender Equality;
(f) the Marketing Committee;
(g) the Sports and Environment Committee.

a. The National Para Olympic Committee, the National Sports Federation for Disabled and the Special Olympics International Greece

174. In Article 29 of the law 2725/1999, as amended, there are certain provisions for the organization of sport for the disabled. It is foreseen that all kinds of sport activities for the disabled are under the protection of the State as follows: sport for the disabled is structured in principle on the basis of sport associations as described above, with some exceptions such as the possibility of the athletes to become members of sport associations. An association for disabled athletes may be considered sports if it has at least ten athletes. At least five associations for disabled athletes may establish a federation for the disabled.

175. The National Para Olympic Committee is the national institution that represents Greece in the I.P.C., has all the goals mentioned in Article 29, paragraph 9 of law 2725/1999 and is administrated as foreseen in that article.

176. Article 29A introduced by law 4908/2022, includes provisions for the function of the sport association called Special Olympics International Greece, which is considered a sports federation for people with mental disability.

II. Professional Sport Organizations

A. *Sections of Paid Athletes*

1. General

177. Professional sport in Greece has two levels: the strictly professional, where the clubs are limited (joint stock) companies (societes anonymes) and the athletes are professional and the semi-professional, where the athletes are called paid athletes and belong to the TAA of sport associations. This semi-professional level is the intermediary phase between the amateur and the professional sport, applying especially in sports that are not amateur but do not fulfil the requirements to be professional. TAA does not have a legal personality but functions as a department of the association, usually independent in the decision-making process but still connected to the association in all representation, tax, insurance and legal responsibility matters. For this reason, the provision for the existence of TAA has been severely

200. Goals of the AAE are forming, organizing and administering the professional team, organizing friendly or official matches and participating in any kind of sport events related to the sport exercised by the team, according to the regulations, goals and decisions of the relevant professional league or the relevant sport federation. The statute of the AAE accepts without reservations and explicitly the statutes of the above institutions, as well as the regulations and the decisions of the higher sport authorities concerning playing and athletic issues, according to Article 65 of law 2725/1999.

201. The founding association (amateur club) plays an important role in the function of the AAE. Law provides that it is obliged to offer its name and logo for the use of the limited company (Article 66), but it cannot offer its sports facilities as participation in the capital because the sports facilities must be granted for use by the AAE with a rental agreement against a rent to be agreed, but should not be smaller than the rent of the public facilities (Article 67). A newly inserted Article (67A) provides that the limited sports company may finance or assign the construction of new facilities or the reconstruction of the old ones upon agreement with the association and permission of the Committee for Professional Sports. Law also provides that in exchange for the offer of name and logo, the amateur club is entitled to receive and always keep 10% of the shares of the limited company against no fee (so only 90% of the capital is offered to shareholder) and to receive 10% of the net income of the limited company from home matches (Article 71). The AAE also undertakes all obligations of the TAA or the respective team of the association which achieved the right to participate in the professional division (Article 73). Finally, the founding association has the right to appoint one member to the Board of Administration of the AAE (Article 74, paragraph 1).

202. The seat of the AAE must be the same as the seat of the founding association (Article 66). Any change of the seat of the AAE requires a licence from the EEA and a positive opinion from the relevant professional league, according to Article 66, paragraph 3.

203. The limited sports companies are governed by the general assembly of their shareholders, to which shares vote and not natural or legal persons. This means that if one person holds more than 50% of the shares, he/she has 50% of the votes in the General Assembly. For the everyday business responsible is the Board of Administration which has as many members as the statutes of the company provide, and the General Assembly elects for a term of no more than six years, which is freely renewable.

204. The AAEs are supervised by the Minister of Development for issues having to do with the forming and the modification of their statutes and by the Deputy Minister of Sport and the EEA for issues having to do with the sport law and their sport activity, according to Article 75 of law 2725/1999.

205. The law also provides in Article 76 the possibility of a merger of two AAEs upon permission of the EEAs.

3. Shareholders, Limitations and Impediments

206. Shareholders of the AAEs can only be individuals of Greek or EU nationality, institutions of the public sector, Greek companies or Greek legal entities of private law and companies or legal entities that have been founded according to the legislation of any Member State of the EU and have their seat or their main administration of settlement in any Member State of the EU, according to Article 69, paragraph 1 of law 2725/1999, as amended several times. Non-EU citizens or legal entities seated outside the EU may acquire shares only after being controlled and obtain a licence from the EEA.

207. The limited companies as well as other legal entities of private law can buy shares only if they obtain the required licence from the EEA (Article 69, paragraphs 2 and 3 as amended). In order to obtain the licence, they must present their full membership status, including all individuals involved as members or shareholders or directors in legal entities involved as members or shareholders.

208. The AAEs are obliged to announce to the EEAs every transfer of shares as well as every change in the names of natural persons involved as members or shareholders or directors in the legal persons who are shareholders.

209. Apart from the above limitations, the sport law sets out some further limitations and impediments for the acquisition of shares of AAEs regarding the athletes on active service, the coaches, the referees, the supervisors of the referees, the intermediaries of Article 90, paragraph 9 (players' and coaches' agents) of law 2725/1999, the husbands and wives of all the above and their first and second-degree relatives (Article 69, paragraph 8). The purchase of shares from the abovementioned people is considered invalid.

210. Furthermore, shareholders of AAEs, members of presidents of a legal entity of private law or of a company participating in the capital of an AAE, their husbands and wives and their first and second-degree relatives are not allowed to acquire directly or indirectly (via intermediaries) shares or power of administration, nor are they allowed to take on managerial tasks of another AAE of the same or of a different branch of sport. An exception to the above limitation is foreseen in case of a person being, i.e., a shareholder of one football and one basketball company originating from the same amateur association (club), which is acceptable.

211. Managers, members of the instruments of administrations, head managers of AAEs, their husbands and wives and their first and second-degree relatives are neither allowed to acquire, directly or indirectly, shares or positions of administrations nor are they allowed to assume managerial tasks of another AAE of the same or of a different branch of sport. People who have undertaken the financial management of the TAA or people who are members or managers of these legal entities are also not allowed to buy shares or to take up managerial tasks of AAEs of another founding sport association or even to participate as members or managers in legal entities or companies that are shareholders of such an AAE. Any act signed despite the above limitations is invalid. The same exception for involvement in sport companies originated from the same amateur association stands for this limitation.

212. If there are violations of the above limitations, for which is responsible the AAE itself, the EEAs imposes an administrative fine and submits the file to the competent sports disciplinary authorities to impose the sanction of deduction of points as well as to the competent criminal authorities (Article 69, paragraphs 12 and 13).

213. For transfers of shares, with which an individual or a body corporate acquires in total a percentage of 5% or more of the stock capital, it is required the licence of the EEA (Article 69A of law 2725/1999, as amended several times). This licence is granted according to the provisions of Article 77, paragraph 5 of law 2725/1999. In order to acquire this licence, the interested one has to hand in to the EEA: (a) tax and insurance awareness, (b) copy of the police record of the interested part, (c) certified copies of the tax statements or the balance sheets of the last three years, and (d) certification of the Committee of Sport Spirit (EFIP) that he has never been punished himself, or in case of a body corporate, its legal representatives (Articles 69 and 130 of law 2725/1999).

214. For transfers of shares, with which an individual or a body corporate acquires in total a percentage of 33% or more of the stock capital, it is additionally required in order to obtain the licence of the EEA three-year business plan, certified by an independent P.D.A. company, including plans of action for the AAE.

4. Professional Leagues of the Sport: Limited Companies – EEA

215. The institutions for the organization of the official competitions of professional character are the sport professional leagues, the members of which are exclusively the AAEs. These leagues, foreseen in Articles 96–118 of law 2725/1999, have their own legal personality as associations or partnerships and enjoy an administrative and managerial autonomy with reference to the respective sport federation, which concerns their internal organization and function. The president of the Board of Administration of each professional league represents the league to the Board of Administration of the respective federation, while the respective federation is represented in the organs of the professional league by an authorized Board member. The statutes and the regulations of the professional leagues are subject to the control of legality by the Deputy Minister of Sport, following an opinion of the respective federation. Among the competencies of the professional league are the organization, administration, and management of the professional championship within the framework of the rules, decisions and goals of the sport federation, the organization and the operation of the events entrusted to it, the institution of disciplinary rules and the resolution of any matter arising from the operation of the championship.

216. According to law 2725/1999, as amended, there are three professional sport leagues:

(1) The League of Professional Football of National Division A (Super League 1 – www.slgr.gr), under the legal form of partnership, the goal of which is the administration and the management of professional football of the highest division within the framework of the football federation, its decisions and regulations and according to the provisions of the sport law. Another goal is the organization of the professional championships of that division, the representation of the participating PAEs in front of the HFF and other authorities, the management of the right for the advertising exploitation and promotion of their activities and the representation of the league in the signing of contracts for the broadcasting of the games or of snapshots of them (Articles 97, 97, 98, 99, paragraphs 1, 100, 101, 101A, 101B, 101C and 101D).

(2) The League of Professional Football of National Division B (Super League 2 – www.sl2.gr), the goal of which is similar in relation to the organization of the championship of the National Division B and the representation of the participating teams (Articles 97, 98, 99, 100, 101, 101A, 101B, 101C, and 101D). Following an amendment of 2021 (Article 20 of law 4809/2021, which amended Article 108 of law 2725/1999), the third national division of football, previously called Football League 2 (while Super League 2 was called Football League 1), became amateur. Article 56 of law 4809/2021 introduced a new Article 108B in law 2725/1999, according to which PAEs participating in Super League 1 may participate with their second team (Team B) in Super League 2 or lower amateur divisions according to the provisions of the regulations of the respective federation.

(3) The Greek League of Basketball Limited Companies (ESAKE – www.esake.gr), the goal of which is identical to the above in relation to the national basketball championship of the highest division (A1) and the participating limited companies (Articles 103, 104, 105, 106 and 107).

217. The sport professional leagues are the connective link between the AAEs and the athletic system, as it is expressed through the function of the federations. The professional leagues function on the basis of the rules, the decisions and the goals of the sport federations. They are administered by the General Assembly and the Board of Administration, which is composed of one representative per member company, who must be its President or Vice-President or owner of at least 10% of its shares (Article 101–101A). The term of office of the Board of Administration of the professional leagues lasts two years. In the frame of each professional league, a separate First Degree One Member Disciplinary Organ function is appointed and competent for disputes according to the provisions of the law and the regulations of the respective federation and league.

218. As already mentioned, in 2006, another professional league was founded following the same standards, the ESAP, according to Article 107A of law 2725/1999, added with law 3479/2006. The main difference from the rest is that its members are not AAE but the volleyball TAA of the A1 division.

C. Common Managerial and Financial Obligations of AAE and TAA Impediments Concerning the Members of the Administration

219. There are a number of common provisions in the TAA and the AAE regarding their financial and managerial obligations, the impediments of the members of their administration, as well as their rights for the electronic broadcasting of the games (Articles 78–84 of law 2725/1999).

220. Before each season begins, the AAE and the TAA must submit to the EEA a balanced budget of incomes and expenses for the new season, together with a credit letter from a bank equal to at least 5% of the budget, according to Article 78, paragraph 1 of law 2725/1999 as amended. Besides, they must have paid off all their due debts to the tax and social authorities, to the professional league and federation they belong, to the athletes and coaches they employ, or they have employed in the past, to the founding sport association and to the owners of sport halls. At the end of each trimester, since the beginning of the championship, the AAE and the TAA are obliged to submit an analytical chart with all their incomes and expenses during the last period (Article 78, paragraph 3).

221. The AAE and the TAA are obliged to make known to the EEA all the amounts of money they receive from members of their administration or from shareholders or from anybody else as a loan or temporary cash facility, according to Article 79, paragraph 1. The notification is made in writing, and it includes: (a) the decision of the competent instrument for the acceptance of the money, (b) the full data of the person who gave the money, and (c) the kind, the height, the purpose and the time for the paying off of the received amount of money (Article 79, paragraph 2). If this information is not notified, both the AAE and the TAA and the members of their administration are personally responsible for the payment of the abovementioned amounts, according to Article 79, paragraph 3. The total amount every AAE may receive as a loan or temporary cash facility may not exceed 20% of its share capital (Article 79, paragraph 4).

222. Finally, the TAA and the AAE are obliged to keep a bank account in a recognized bank and to hand in the relevant bank documents whenever they are asked for from the EEA and the General Secretariat for Sport, according to Article 81 of law 2725/1999.

223. Any person who has one of the impediments set out for his participation in the sport associations, or any person that has been peremptorily punished by the EFIP and for as long as this punishment lasts, is not allowed to become a member of the administration of an AAE or TAA (Article 3, paragraph 1 and Article 83). Otherwise, this person automatically loses his position. This is ascertained by the competent judicial instrument following a report of the EEA. For this reason, the AAE and the TAA are obliged to submit to the EEA a legal statement of each member of their administration, declaring that no impediment succours to their person and, within a month, a copy of their police record (Article 83, paragraph 3). If they fail to hand in the copy of the police record, the member of the Board of Administration loses his post following an ascertaining decision of the relevant judicial instrument (Article 83, paragraph 4). The AAE or the TAA must comply with this decision within ten days of its notification. If it fails to comply with it, its team is expelled from the championship with a decision of the relevant judicial instrument, according to Article 83, paragraph 5 of law 2725/1999. In case the AAE or TAA allows individuals who had been members of the administration and then were deposed with a peremptory decision of the relevant judicial instrument to participate in the instruments of their administrations, they are punished with the loss of the points of the victory for every game of the championship and for as long as this illegal omission lasts, according to Article 80. The Board members and the shareholders of at least 1% of the capital of an AAE must also submit on a yearly basis to the competent statal authority a declaration of their financial situation aiming to justify their fortune according to their sources of income (Article 83, paragraph 3).

224. According to Article 118A of law 2725/1999, as amended, all persons who administer sport legal entities are jointly responsible with the legal entity for the payment of every taxation connected with the activity of the legal entity. Presidents, directors, managers, CEOs or other administrators of the AAE or TAA or association participating in professional championships are also jointly responsible for any debt of the legal entity to anyone, including debts to athletes, coaches, etc.

III. Sport Facilities

225. Sport facilities (stadiums, sport halls, swimming pools, etc.) can be public, municipal or private. Although in the past, most of them were public, today only a few still are, such as the Agios Kosmas Sports Center in Athens and the Alexandrio Sport Hall in Thessaloniki. The Athens Olympic Stadium and the Peace and Friendship Stadium in Athens have a legal personality of private law, but they are administrated by the State. Kaftantzogleio Stadium in Thessaloniki has another peculiar legal status, because it belongs to a Foundation, but is also administrated by the State. The majority of the sport facilities belong to the local authorities of the place where they are installed (i.e., municipality), thus having a public legal personality of a different kind, and only a few of them are private, belonging to sports associations or private natural or legal persons.

226. Aiming to ensure public safety and security, law 2725/1999 after several amendments contains a series of provisions for the periodical control, the licensing and the categorization of sports facilities and the permission to hold sports events, which must be obtained for every event individually (Articles 56, 56A, 56B, 56C, 56D and 57) including a provision to initiate criminal procedure leading to imprisonment of at least three months and fine to anyone who permits or organizes a sport event in breach of the above.

227. A AAE, a TAA or a sport association that has rent areas of any public, municipal or private sport facility has the exclusive right to exploit the advertising areas during the friendly or the official events, regardless of the fact that these events may be broadcasted by the television, according to Article 56, paragraphs 1 and 2 of law 2725/1999. The transfer of the use of the above right is only allowed with a contract among the owner or the hirer of the sport facility, the host AAE or TAA or association or federation and the individual or the body corporate to whom the right is transferred. The AAE, TAA or association is obliged to pay the owner or the hirer a percentage of at least 15% of the total cost of the abovementioned contract (Article 56, paragraph 3). The payment is directly executed by the individual or the body corporate to which the transfer of the use was agreed and is then deducted from what the individual or the body corporate owes to the tenant.

228. The contract between a PAE competing in the highest division of the professional championship and the owner of national, municipal or associational sport facilities is allowed on condition that the tenant PAE is charged with the expenses for the maintenance of the grass field. It is also possible that this contract sets out the transfer of the use of the grass field. Furthermore, a contract that has as an object the commercial exploitation of the free areas of the sport facilities, which are not supposed to be used for other goals, is also allowed.

Chapter 2. Public Regulation

§1. Fundamental Rights – The Application of Constitutional Provisions in Sport[8]

I. Human Value (Article 2, Paragraph 1 of the Constitution)

229. As already mentioned, the Constitution of the Hellenic Republic refers to physical education and sports in two points. Article 16, paragraph 2 stipulates physical education as one of the main missions of the State, the goal of which is the making of free and responsible citizens and Article 16, paragraph 9 makes clear reference to sport activity and establishes the role of the State in the protection, the supervision and the control of sport institutions. There are much more fundamental constitutional rights, though, that apply directly or indirectly in sports activity.

230. According to Article 2, paragraph 1 of the Constitution, the respect and protection of human value constitute the major obligation of the State. This way, the human value, which is the set of the general, material, spiritual and social features of a human being, is protected.

231. In the sport field, both the State and all those who are occupied with the sport phenomenon are obliged to protect the athletes' human value. This constitutional provision must be the gnomon for the regulation of the sport activity for every competent institution in a way that serves the needs of the human nature of the athletes. In the field of professional sport, the application of this principle commands the respect of human nature from different sport institutions, especially with reference to their goal for the achievement of the best sport result possible and, through it, the achievement of the greatest financial benefit possible. The purchase and the sale of athletes according to the system of transfers, the doping phenomenon, with its harming consequences on the athletes' health, and the estimation of the athlete's value for logistical purposes (Article 76A of law 2725/1999 as amended several times so far), etc., could be considered violations of this constitutional provision but should be examined only in the frame of specificity of sport.

II. Equality (Article 4 of the Constitution)

232. Article 4 of the Constitution introduced the principle of equality of the citizens in front of the law. The principle of equality is a fundamental constitutional provision appearing in all the fields of the legal order. It is applied under two forms: the positive one, which is the principle of equal treatment, and the negative one, which is the prohibition of discrimination.

8. Elements in this chapter have been taken from the work of A. Malatos, *Lessons of Sports Law*, 2005, 115, etc.

233. In the sport field, the principle of equality, both as a defensive and as a protective right, may be applied against the State and/or against the authority of the sport associations and federations, founding the right of every athlete for a fair and equal treatment on behalf of the sport institutions. The prohibition of bribery for the alteration of a game result and the prohibition of doping constitute characteristic cases where this principle may find application.

234. In the field of equality, there are cases of women who want to participate in sport activity, either professionally or as amateurs. The principle of equality between men and women in the sport field applies to the obligation of the State and the sport institutions not only to allow but also to facilitate the participation of women in the sports they cultivate. A special provision also exists for the obligation of participation of persons from both sexes in the Board of Administration of the sports federations, although its application is limited due to the requirement for the existence of a certain number of candidates from each sex without consequences in case of a breach.

235. This constitutional principle may also be applied to people who need special treatment, such as handicapped people. Article 21, paragraph 2 of the Constitution establishes the right of people with corporal or mental disabilities to special treatment from the State. The legislator must take all the necessary measures for the protection of the above people.

236. The application of this principle with reference to disabled people basically constitutes the care that must be shown by the sport institutions for these athletes, a care which is fulfilled with the organization of special games, with the foundation of sport association for disabled people (Article 29 of law 2725/1999 as amended) and with the general organization and function of sport activity for these people.

237. Finally, it is worth mentioning that the honorary titles set out by the law (Article 2, paragraphs 1 and 34 of law 2725/1999, i.e., nomination of honorary members, giving of prizes and medals, etc.) are compatible with the constitutional principle of equality and they cannot be considered as prohibited according to Article 4, paragraph 7 of the Constitution. It is the same for the provisions setting out financial benefits and gifts given to athletes that achieve great competitive performances either in individual or team sports (Articles 34 and 35 of law 2725/1999 as amended several times).

III. Free Development of the Personality and Participation in the Economic Life (Article 5 Paragraph 1 of the Constitution)

238. According to Article 5, paragraph 1 of the Constitution, everyone has the right to develop his personality and to participate in the social, economic, and political life of the country, on condition that he does not harm the other citizens' right and he does not violate the Constitution or the moral ethos. This way, the free development of personality, i.e., human freedom, is secured as an objective principle and a fundamental right.

239. The Constitution explicitly secures the abovementioned freedom by recognizing separate rights, the rights of participation in the social, economic, and political life of the country. Free participation in the sport activity is also included in the meaning of this constitutional provision. Participation in the sport activity as a social activity not only serves the free development of the human personality but also contributes to the formation of the cultural, social, and economic life of the country. The free choice of sport, the freedom to exercise and to train, the freedom of entrance to the sport facilities, and the free participation in the sport institutions belong to the framework of the free development of personality through sport.

240. Therefore, according to the provision of Article 5, paragraph 1 of the Constitution, in the sport field, the State must secure the free development of the sport abilities of every athlete and take care of the free and easy access to sport facilities and organizations. Limitations of this right can only be accepted to the extent that the Constitution and the law allow them for reasons of protection of the sport phenomenon and public interest. Limitations of such kind are, for example, the infliction of disciplinary sanctions on those who refuse to participate in the national teams, according to Article 33, paragraph 5 of law 2725/1999, the obligation of certification of the athletes' good state of health according to Article 33, paragraph 9 of law 2725/1999, the prohibition of the use of doping substances according to Article 128A, etc.

241. Another case of limitation to the free development of the personality in the sport field is the provision of Article 130, paragraph 2 of law 2725/1999 for the privation of the sport quality. This limitation has been set out with the aim of protecting the sport spirit from incidents that damage the sport phenomenon.

242. Absolutely compatible with the free development of the personality is the right of every athlete to choose the sport association of his preference in order to be able to take part in one or more sports, as well as the limitations, terms and conditions for the registration and the transfer of the athletes, set out in regulations of the sport federations foreseen in Article 27 of the law 2725/1999, although ASEAD has accepted in some cases that some of these limitations are against this constitutional provision. It must be recognized though that recently, an amendment has been introduced according to which all athletes above 18 years old may freely transfer every season to another association of their choice.

243. The sector of economic freedom, both as an individual right and as a principle of the legal order, has a special meaning in the field of the sport activity because of the special features of the sport phenomenon and due to its monopolistic and hierarchically structured organization. The immense social interest in the sport activity in the last decades has rendered it an important financial human activity since one part of it has been transformed into paid and professional sport activity. Therefore, within the framework of this constitutional provision, the legislator is expected to balance and apply harmonically both the sport – ideological and the commercial – financial dimensions of the sport activity. The rules set out by the State for the regulation of betting and other similar activities related to the sport, constitute nowadays a field of special interest for sports law.

IV. Privacy: Residence Asylum (Article 9, Paragraph 1 of the Constitution)

244. The Constitution protects the residence and the private and family life of the citizens with Article 9, paragraph 1, defining that: 'Everybody's residence is an asylum. The private and family life of everyone cannot be trespassed. No survey can take place in a private residence unless the law permits it and always with the presence of representatives of the judiciary authority.'

245. Bearers of this right are the athletes as well, since they are well-known people and because their family and private life may be trespassed or limited due to the interest the public may show for them. Publications, information, and photos of athletes may constitute a violation of their privacy, which is secured by the relevant constitutional provision. Nevertheless, their right to privacy may be limited for reasons of public interest through the free information with printed or electronic means. Other limitations concerning the family life of athletes may also be permitted in case athletes are obliged to follow their teams on long-lasting trips, during which they are not accompanied by their families.

246. The residence is also protected in the same way. The constitutionally protected residence is the place the athlete can deny or permit access to. Residence is not only the house or the building but also any area which is fenced in such a way that the access to it is not free. Thus, the area, the destination of which is the exercise of the sport activities (events, trainings), may under these conditions also be considered as a constitutionally protected area. In the areas above, the intervention of exterior authorities may be prohibited unless the law permits it, always with the presence of representatives of the judiciary authority. Other interventions, without the presence of the judiciary representatives, such as the obligation to provide whereabouts information and the sudden doping controls carried out by WADA, NADO, International Federation, National Federation or any other competent authority, could be considered constitutionally problematic but lately it is accepted that they constitute limitations necessarily imposed to protect sports integrity.

V. Freedom of Gatherings (Article 11 of the Constitution)

247. Article 11 of the Constitution protects gatherings. The type of gathering protected by the Constitution is a peaceful and unarmed concentration or meeting of people at a specific time and place, public or private, with the same goal.

248. Simple gatherings need no protection since the concentration of people happens at random, without previous communication and with different goals from the goals a protected gathering may have. Besides, in a protected gathering, there is a common goal for all the participants, contrary to a random concentration of people.

249. As far as the freedom of gathering within the sport fields in Greece is concerned, there are doubts about whether the sport gatherings constitute a gathering in the sense of a constitutionally protected gathering. It has been supported in the past that the accumulation of people in a sport facility at a specific time and place, during a sport meeting, is random. It is a simple concentration of people for entertaining reasons, without a community or unity of goals therefore it does not constitute the sense of gathering defined by the relevant constitutional provision.

250. The above point of view does not seem reasonable nowadays since it is commonplace that today there is a previous communication among the organized fans of the leagues of fans, to arrange their presence during the sport meeting. For this reason, it must be accepted that there is the necessary element of the community of goal among the abovementioned fans since they enter the sport facility not only to watch the match but also demonstrate in an active and organized way their support to the team or to the athletes.

251. Besides, we must consider that the sport facility, where the sport meeting takes place, is usually a closed or fenced place, so that access to it is not possible from everywhere. The fact that a lot of people enter it without their being known in advance makes this gathering a public gathering, even if people have to pay a ticket in order to enter the sport facility and watch the match.

252. The ascertainment that the sport meetings are public and closed gatherings has a special importance for the possibility of banning them. The authorization given by the Constitution to the police to attend or ban a gathering (Article 11, paragraph 2 of the Constitution) is limited only to the public outdoor gatherings.

253. It must be clear, however, that the presence of a police force and any preventive or suppressive measure taken by the police during a sport meeting is not contrary to the constitutional provision of Article 11, paragraph 1. On the contrary, it helps the materialization of it, taking into consideration that in fact the police are invited by the organizers of the game themselves for reasons of security and protection from violent behaviours and from vandal acts committed by the so-called hooligans, whose goal is not just to watch the match and support their team, but actually to destroy the sport meeting with curses, abuses and attacks on other spectators, referees and athletes, even with the use of items able to subtract from the sport meeting its peaceful, unarmed and socially beneficial role.

254. Such kinds of limitations are set out in the sport law 2725/1999 (provisions regarding the sport violence in Article 41Γ, 41Δ and 41E as amended several times) and the ratified Convention of the European Council for the Sport Violence.

VI. Freedom of Associating (Article 12 of the Constitution)

255. According to Article 12, paragraph 1 of the Constitution, the citizens have the right to form unions and non-profiteering associations. The exercise of this right does not depend on a previous licence.

256. A union of people, which is protected by Article 12 of the Constitution, is every formal or informal permanent union which has a non-profiteering goal, in which every individual may participate or not without any previous licence but only after the judiciary confirmation of its legitimacy.

257. Such kinds of unions are of course the sport associations, which are specially ruled by Article 16, paragraph 9 of the Constitution. This constitutional provision sets out the public support of the sport association through a control system different from the one exercised and imposed on the rest of the common unions and associations. The public allocations and the public control of the sport associations are directly set out in the Constitution itself. In this framework, the provisions of Articles 1–30 of law 2725/1999, which describe the administrative supervision of sport associations, unions and federations, are absolutely compatible with the Constitution.

258. Furthermore, the freedom of unions and associations set out in the Constitution includes the freedom to enter or exit a sport association, union or federation, the right to participate in their function and the freedom to define their goal. These freedoms may be limited only within the framework set out by Article 16, paragraph 9 of the Constitution.

VII. Religious Freedom (Article 13 of the Constitution)

259. According to Article 13 of the Constitution, the freedom of religious beliefs cannot be violated. The exercise of individual and political rights does not depend on religious beliefs.

260. The abovementioned freedom cannot be violated in the field of sport. Such kind of violation could be the prohibition of entrance into sport facilities for people who believe in a certain religion or support a certain dogma, or even the enforcement of a religious oath to those occupied with sports. Discrimination against athletes because of their religious beliefs is not allowed, and lately, more and more sports federations have included in their disciplinary regulations,' provisions of heavy sanctions for racist behaviour which definitely includes discrimination due to nationality or religion.

VIII. Freedom of Press (Article 14 of the Constitution)

261. According to Article 14, paragraph 1 of the Constitution, everyone can express and circulate orally, written or through the press his thoughts, by observing the laws of the State. According to Article 14, paragraph 2 of the Constitution, press is free, and censorship and any other preventive measure are forbidden. According to paragraph 3, the confiscation of printed matters either before or after their circulation is not allowed except for the special suppressive confiscation imposed by the Constitution, only at a prosecutor's command. In the meaning of press, we should definitely include the internet as a means of transfer of ideas and opinions.

262. Sport press also enjoys the guarantees of Article 14 of the Constitution. In Greece, some sport newspapers are still published daily, and many sports websites and blogs are focused on the sport activity. Press is free to spread ideas and opinions regarding the sport activity. Censorship, confiscation, and any other suppressive measure against the sport press is forbidden. A few constitutionally accepted exceptions are set out in the sport law 2725/1999 (Article 41, paragraph 2), which bans public statements that may disturb the peaceful organization of the sport meetings or bring about tension among sport fans. Statements and behaviours expressed through the press (including electronic press, blogs, etc.) that lead to the perpetration of acts of violence are punished, according to Article 41F, paragraph 5 of law 2725/1999.

IX. Freedom of Radio and Television (Article 15 of the Constitution)

263. Article 15 of the Constitution regulates the radio, the television, the cinema and other relevant means of circulation and broadcasting of information, speech or picture.

264. Article 15 has a particular meaning about the sport programs and the exclusiveness of telecasting of sport events, especially within the framework of private television.

265. The right of the exclusive telecasting and transmission of sport events has acquired a legal interest because of the increase of the financial activity in sport after the gigantism of the Olympic Games and other major sports events, such as the world or continental championships.

266. Regarding the Olympic Games or other international events, it is worth mentioning that the IOC and the international federations are the only possessors of all the rights having to do with the transmission and the telecasting of them, and they sell those rights to the organizers or directly to TV channels according to certain agreements.

267. For the sport events of national range, the right for their broad- and telecasting is set out by the relevant provisions of Article 84 and 84A of the sport law 2725/1999 as amended. In principle, those rights for team sports belong to the home team, except for cup matches and national team matches, which belong to the national federation and the Super League 2 matches which by law (Article 84A) belong to the Super League. Article 84 includes a provision that for sports events of major interest, as defined by a ministerial decree issued regularly, an obligation exists to be transmitted by free-to-air channels.

X. The Right for Education (Article 16 of the Constitution)

268. Article 16 defines education as a basic objective for the State, and it has as a goal the moral, spiritual, professional and physical education of the citizens, the development of their moral conscience and the forming of free and responsible persons. Education, as an individual right, includes physical education as well. The bearer of this constitutional right has a demand from the State for the support of his physical, athletic, and gymnastic education.

269. Concerning the fulfilment of this right, the legislator sets out the organization of school games and the incorporation of the physical education (gym) in the program of the obligatory education of primary, secondary and high schools. It also regulates the function of public and private gymnasiums and sport halls. Finally, the legislator cares for the development of school sport and for the combination with the associational sport (Article 58 of law 2725/1999). Recently, the need for education of all people involved in sports governance as another aspect of the right to education has been recognized, and the need for a legal provision of it has been raised. Such provision has been included in drafts of new sports law but has not been realized yet.

XI. The Right for Property (Article 17 of the Constitution)

270. Property is under the protection of the State, but the rights resulting from it cannot be exercised against the public interest. The Constitution sets limits to the private property with the institution of the obligatory expropriation. Regarding the application of the relevant constitutional provision in the field of sport, a kind of public interest, which could lead to the privation of property through an obligatory expropriation, are the public projects for the creation of sport facilities, sport fields, gymnasiums, etc. This privation can only take place after the payment of the relevant remuneration to the owners of the property deprived of the materialization of the abovementioned public plans. This constitutional provision was especially applied during the preparation of the Olympic works.

XII. Protection of the Childhood (Article 21, Paragraph 1 of the Constitution)

271. Article 21 of the Constitution sets out that the family, as a cornerstone for the preservation and the promotion of the Nation, as well as marriage, motherhood and childhood, fall under the protection of the State.

272. Taken for granted that the sport quality is usually acquired under the age of 18, the protection of the childhood set out in different ways by the sport law 2725/1999 (Articles 3, 7, 34, 35, 90, etc.) has a special interest within the framework of Article 21, paragraph 1 of the Constitution. Taking into consideration that young athletes are in a phase of development of their personality, the obligation on behalf of the State to protect them is critical since the heavy and increased obligations of the athletes nowadays can limit this development and harm it.

273. The constitutional protection of the childhood imposes the taking of measures against anti-pedagogic treatment and especially against the financial or any other kind of exploitation of young athletes, e.g., with the use of doping substances, the increase of the training time at the expense of other activities, with the exhausting training and with the abuse of the power exercised on a child by his trainer, coach, etc.

XIII. Right for Health and for Genetic Identity (Article 21, Paragraphs 3 and 5 of the Constitution)

274. Health is the physical, corporal, and spiritual state of a person. The constitutional provisions concerning health are rather important for sport today because of the strenuous and exhausting training many athletes are subject to, training that may even damage their health.

275. Law 2725/1999 entrusts the training of athletes to expert trainers and university graduates who have special knowledge of physical education and special qualifications.

276. The securing of the athletes' health is a very important issue, and the certification of its good state is compulsory for their participation in the games, according to Article 33, paragraph 9 of law 2725/1999. Paragraph 2 of the same article contains provisions for the insurance of amateur athletes and Article 89 for the insurance of paid and professional athletes. Article 36, paragraph 4 of law 2725/1999, also contains a provision for free hospital coverage for amateur athletes who are not directly or indirectly insured by some private or public insurance company.

277. A possible problem that may arise with the implementation of the constitutional provisions protecting the athletes' health is in the case of the clauses included in the sport contracts between an athlete and a sport federation. These clauses may impose a certain doctor on the athlete, subtracting this way his right to freely choose a doctor of his own preference. Such kinds of clauses may be against the Constitution under certain circumstances but should always be examined under the specificity of sport.

XIV. The Right for Work and Social Insurance (Article 22 of the Constitution)

278. Article 22 of the Constitution establishes the right to work for every citizen. This constitutional right, incorporated in the institutional framework of sport, has a particular content, which is characterized by the problem of establishment of the professional freedom of paid and professional athletes. Professional freedom is identical to the freedom of work, which guarantees that everybody can choose the kind, the place and the duration of his work, as well as the means and the ways of his professional activity. The fact that the sport labour relation is ruled by both the public and the sport legislation creates a special legal interest.

279. A special legal interest is also caused by the fact that compulsory work is constitutionally forbidden. In this framework, the system of the athletes' transfer and the binding of the athletes to their team may be considered problematic, taking into account the relevant constitutional provision, since this binding actually abolishes the athlete's freedom to choose his employer.

280. The Constitution also includes a provision regarding social insurance, establishing it as an institution and defining that a simple law has its content. This constitutional provision has been realized in the field of sports law with Article 89 of law 2725/1999, which regulates the insurance of athletes.

XV. Unionist Freedom: Strike (Article 23 of the Constitution)

281. The Constitution establishes the unionist freedom in Article 23, paragraph 1, defining that the State has to take all the necessary measures to secure the unionist freedom and the unhindered exercise of the relevant rights against any violation within the framework of the law.

282. The bearer of the unionist right may also be the athlete. The athletes have the right to establish syndicates and to pursue their rights through these syndicates. They also have the right to go on a strike, according to Article 23, paragraph 2 of the Constitution, which defines that the strike is a right exercised by the legal trade unions for the protection and the amelioration of the financial and working interests of the employees. The same stands for the coaches who as foreseen in Article 31 of the law 2725/1999 participate in one national association per sport.

XVI. Protection of the Environment (Article 24 of the Constitution)

283. The protection of the environment is actually the protection of the existence and the health of the man himself.

284. As far as the field of sport is concerned, the main threat to the environment is human activities and interventions resulting in environmental alterations for the creation of sport facilities. These human interventions should not cause irreversible damage to the environment, even if the sport phenomenon is also protected by the Constitution. The parallel protection of the environment and sport may lead to an inevitable limitation of one right at the expense of the other.

XVII. The Judiciary Constitutional Rights (Article 5, Paragraph 3 and Articles 6, 7, 8 and 20 of the Constitution)

285. Article 5, paragraph 3 and Articles 6 and 7 of the Constitution include some 'traditional provisions,' the goal of which is the protection of the citizens against the arbitrary acts of the State power, mainly in the framework of the penal prosecution, by establishing the prohibition of the arbitrary arrest, imprisonment and of any other limitation of the natural freedom and by securing the principle 'no crime and no penalty without a law set out before the commitment of the crime and describing exactly the crime'.

286. The principles formed by the abovementioned provisions can have application in the field of the sport law, not only in the vital area of sport but also as principles and axioms for the production and the implementation of the private disciplinary law of the sport federations on athletes and associations.

287. Since the law does not exist outside the sport life, the intervention of the judge is not only allowed but also necessary for the securing of the normal rhythm of sport life, for the existence of good relations among the participants in the sport life and for the public peace in the field of sport. The subjects of the sport legal order have in principle the right to resolve their disputes in the regular courts. This is a fundamental right of theirs, dictated by Articles 8 and 20 of the Constitution and by Article 6 of the European Convention for Human Rights.

288. However, sports organizations internationally tend to apply their own judicial system of dispute resolution of an arbitral nature and to prohibit natural or legal persons subject to them to address to normal courts by signing declarations containing such clauses in order to obtain the right to participate in sport competitions. The foundation of these instruments, their competencies and their function are also governed by the abovementioned constitutional provisions, even if these instruments do not constitute courts in the meaning of the Constitution.

§2. Governmental Conditions and Permits

289. In law 2725, quite many governmental conditions and permits exist proving the excessive interventionism of the State in sports activity without taking into consideration the specificity of sports and the need for self-determination of sports activity and the self – administration pf the sports institutions.

In a non-exhaustive list, such governmental interventions are:

- The deed of dismissal by the competent organ of the General Secretariat of Sport of a Board member of an association who has any of the obstacles or does not fulfil any of the criteria set in Article 3 of law 2725/1999 as well as of the Board members who did not decide his dismissal (Article 3, paragraph 9).
- The obligation that in elections of the Board of Administration of sports associations, there must be candidates from every gender at least equal to one-third of

the places to be covered (Article 5, paragraph 5). A similar provision exists in Article 13, paragraph 3 for sports unions. This intervention is, in practice, only a suggestion because the law does not provide any consequence in case of breach.

- The Special Athletic Recognition for associations, unions and federations (Articles 8, 17, 28) and the Registry of Sports Associations.
- The control of lists of associations with voting rights in the General Assembly of a sports union or federation by the General Secretariat of Sport according to Article 14, paragraph 6 and Article 24 paragraph 2.
- The approval of the regulations of the federations by the Minister of Sport according to Article 27.
- The control of the employees of the federations and their fees according to Article 30.
- The issuance by the General Secretariat of Sports of licence for the profession of sports coach as a necessity to practise it according to Article 31.
- The imposition of terms of establishment and operation of a private gym or a sports school and the control of their operation according to Article 32.
- The financial benefits and facilities to athletes for distinctions according to Article 34.
- The creation of a special care account for amateur athletes, according to Article 36.
- The right of DEAV to impose administrative sanctions like fines and stadium closure in parallel with the competent disciplinary institutions according to Article 41A of the law 2725/1999 and Article 1 and 1A of the law 4326/2015
- The necessity for licence and the control of the operation of fan clubs according to Article 41B.
- The right of the Minister of Sport to decide the postponement of a sports event for security reasons according to Article 41D, paragraph 5.
- The provision of disciplinary sanctions for violent incidents in breach of the provisions of Article 41–41F of the law. This provision, which in practice has never been applied, constitutes the most extreme intervention of the state to the regulations of the federations in order to arrange which should be the disciplinary sanction per breach, disregarding the autonomy of sports.
- The grants of the General Secretariat of Sport to sports institutions supervised by it according to Article 50.
- The obligation for submission of financial statements and budgets of all sports institutions to the General Secretariat of Sport according to Article 51.
- The financial control of supervised institutions as per Article 52.
- The conditions for the issuance of licences for the sports facilities according to Article 56B and 56C and the issuance of permission to hold a sports event according to Article 56D.
- The control and limitations of buying shares in AAEs according to Article 69 and 69A.
- The control of AAEs by the Committee for Professional Sport, including the issuance of a certificate to participate in the competitions according to Article 77 and 77A.
- The control of any payments and loans to the AAEs according to Article 79.

Apart from the above conditions and permits provided in the main sports law, general law provisions, such as work permits for non-EU citizens, apply to players, coaches and other persons involved in sports associations, unions, federations, TAA and limited companies.

§3. Tort Law

I. Disciplinary Offences

290. In the disciplinary regulations of the sports federations, it is defined which kind of behaviour of athletes, coaches, administrators or other persons involved in sport activity is considered unsportsmanlike or against the spirit of sport and, therefore, is disciplinary sanctioned by the competent judicial institution. Usual actions which are considered disciplinary offences are doping, insults, assault and violent behaviour in general, regardless of the damage caused to the victim. The sanctions vary from simple warning to disqualification for one or more matches or for a certain period. In very serious cases, definitive disqualification can be inflicted.

291. It is also worth mentioning that in the disciplinary regulations of the federations, the strict liability rule often applies regarding the responsibility of the associations, TAA or AAEs for the behaviour of their fans, especially when violent incidents take place resulting in the interruption of a match or the injury of any person involved in it.

II. Penal Crimes Committed in Relation to the Sport Activities

292. During sport activity or in connection with it, as well as with any other human activity, some crimes punishable by the PC or special penal laws may be committed. The penal crimes committed in relation to the sport activities are divided into genuine and non-genuine ones.

293. Genuine sport crimes are those that can be committed only before or during a sport event or even because of it. Genuine sport crimes are standardized in the sport law 2725/1999 since the Greek Penal Code does not include any.

294. On the contrary, non-genuine sport crimes are those standardized in the PC or in other penal laws and provisions. They are committed not necessarily in connection with sport activity, but if they take place before, during or because of the sport activity, they may be treated differently. Non-genuine sport crimes can be murder, assault, insult, defamation, fraud and many other crimes that can also be committed in connection with sport activity.

295. The most important genuine sport crimes are: (a) violence in sport (Article 41 ST of law 2725/1999), (b) doping (Article 128 Θ),[9] and (c) bribery committed with the aim of altering a match result (Article 132 of the same law). In law 2725/1999, there is also provision for some other genuine crimes less serious, such as the arbitrary giving of an allocation for a purpose other than it was granted for (Article 50, paragraph 5), the obstruction of the control of the sports institutions by the General Inspector of Public Administration (Article 52A), the refusal of giving documents or information to the EEAs (Article 77A) and the participation in the administration of a TAA or in an AAE against the provisions set in the law (Articles 61 and 69).

III. Violence in Sport

A. *Introduction*

296. Violence is a phenomenon that has existed ever since man was born, and it constitutes a basic, everlasting element of human life in all its forms, e.g., within the family, society, political life, art, religion, etc.[10] Violence is distinguished into purely material (corporal) violence and psychological violence (threat).

297. Sport violence is a form of human violence as well. Although it is not a modern phenomenon, its frequent appearance over the last decades has turned it into a critical sport and social problem, which sport and political authorities worldwide try to deal with and which constitutes the object of study for a lot of sciences, such as the sociology, the psychology, the criminology, the philosophy and the legal sciences.

298. Violence in sport events is demonstrated under two forms, either as violence among the athletes and other participants in a sport event or as violence brought about by the spectators, addressed either to other spectators and fans or to the athletes, the referees and other participants in the sport event.

299. The violence among the athletes and the remaining participants in a sport event appears as the result of the strain and the passion for the game. It can be easily explained if we take into account the wish to reach the victory and due to it to achieve a series of other goods related to the victory. The level of this kind of violence depends on the nature of the sport. So, it is much more likely for incidents of violence to take place during a sport event where the athletes come in close contact with each other (rugby, ice hockey, football, basketball, etc.).

300. The violence caused by the spectators of a sport event, either among them or against some of the participants in the game, such as the athletes, the referees, the policemen, the journalists, etc., is this form of violence that has made it one of

9. Doping will be the subject of analysis below in Part III, paras 526–588.
10. Elements are taken from the work of A. Mavromatis, *Sport Crimes*, 2006, 51, etc.

the most serious problems nowadays. Acts of violence in this category, which contain the element of contempt against people and property, are internationally known as 'hooliganisms'.

301. Contrary to the acts of violence taking place among the participants of a sport game, acts of violence caused by the spectators happen regardless of the kind of the sport event. For instance, while rugby is one of the most violent sports, incidents of violence among the spectators during or before a rugby game are really rare.

302. Violence in the sport fields is not a modern phenomenon. Incidents of violence have been reported in antiquity as well. In ancient Greece, the exercise of violence was acceptable, and sports presupposing the use of violence, such as the 'pigmi' or the 'pagratium,' were at a high social rank. There are also reports of brawls and hand-to-hand fights among the spectators watching the games. Incidents of violence have also been reported in other eras, for example, in Byzantium.

303. In modern Greece, incidents of violence are reported since the decades of 1960s and 1970s. The most serious of these incidents is the damage caused in the field 'Leoforos Alexandras' after a football match between Olympiacos and Panathinaikos when fans of both teams protested in a violent way for the game and the referees. In a football game in Agrinio, some fans cut the referee's ear, while in another football match in Larisa, a person was killed by a flare thrown by the fans of the opposite team. The economic crisis of the last decade caused a flare-up of violence among fans, and in various incidents during the previous years, at least three persons were killed and quite many injured.

304. There are a lot of reasons that can explain the phenomenon of violence in the sport fields. Some of them are:

- Aggression as a structural and not as an accidental or marginal feature of the function and the ideology of modern society.
- Some sociological factors, such as the existence of various and different social and class layers, economic and demographical differentiations, unemployment, racism, and social injustice.
- The grouping of the fans of a team, the fanaticism and the identification of a team's supporters with its athletes due to the abovementioned factors.
- The rules of mass psychology and crowd behaviour. A fanatic supporter feels safe and anonymous in the middle of a crowd that acts and behaves in a spontaneous way that influences him as well.
- A series of other factors, such as the decisions of the organizers of the games or the governmental institutions that create a climate of unreliability, rumours for predefined game results, acts of violence that had taken place between the fans of the same teams in past games, inadequate policing, incendiary publishing in the press, etc.

B. Preventing Measures

305. The Greek law contains many provisions for the confrontation of violence in sport in Article 41–41Z both by taking preventive measures and by defining severe disciplinary and penal sanctions as restraining measures. The respective provisions have been amended several times, especially following serious incidents.

306. For the prevention of sport violence, the following measures have been taken:

- Any person involved under any capacity (athlete, coach, administrative member of association, union or federation, referee, etc.) in sport activity shall refrain from any action or public declaration that may risk causing violent incidents in sport events. The violation of this obligation is disciplinary sanctioned according to the regulations of the relevant federation (Article 41).
- A committee is founded in the General Secretariat of Sport, the DEAV[11] (Article 41A). By law 5085/2024, following the death of a police officer in violent incidents in the end of 2023, competence was given to DEAV to impose administrative sanctions to clubs including stadium closure.
- Special requirements are set for the control of the foundation and the function of the clubs of sport associations' fans, their members and the distribution of tickets to them (Article 41B). Administrative and penal sanctions are foreseen for the violation of the above.
- The measures of issuing electronic numbered tickets with the name of their holders on them, issuing a sport fan card and the definition by the police of certain sections in stadiums for the fans of the participating teams in order to ensure that they do not meet with the fans of the home team risking violent incidents and the distribution of tickets accordingly. Administrative, disciplinary and penal sanctions are foreseen for the violation of these measures, while the Minister of Sport upon introduction of the police has the right to prohibit the distribution of tickets to the fans of the visiting team (Article 41C).[12]
- Before any sport match of high risk for violent incidents, a meeting is organized by the police with the participation of the teams' representatives and the organizing federation or professional league's security responsible person in order to take any other appropriate measure, such as to define the itinerary for the fans of the visiting team to and from the stadium, etc. (Article 41D). Administrative, disciplinary and penal sanctions are foreseen for those who do not conform to the imposed measures and the orders of the competent public authorities.
- Cameras are obligatorily installed in all sport halls where matches of the highest division of football, basketball or volleyball take place (Article 41E).[13]

---

11. *See* above para. 29.
12. Law 5085/2024 amended the respective article by providing serious sanctions to anyone found by the police controls to attend a sport event without ticket in his name and to the clubs that allow fans to enter without ticket or with tickets in the name of other persons.
13. The cameras provisions were also amended by law 5085/2024 which also provides administrative sanctions including stadium closure in case of failure to comply with those provisions.

C. Sport Violence as a Crime

307. The several aspects of sport violence as a penal crime are set in Article 41ST of law 2725/1999 added with law 3057/2002, which replaced the old law 1646/1986 and has been amended several times so far. The crimes of sport violence can be committed by anybody, regardless of the fact that he/she takes part in a sport event as an athlete, coach, administrative member of a sport association, doctor, referee, etc., or that he/she just attends the match as a fan or spectator. This means that both forms of sport violence are punished, e.g., the violence among the participants of a sport event and the violence among the spectators.

308. The main crime, defined in paragraph 1, can be committed in various acts and ways, each one of them being enough to standardize it. These possible ways of committing this crime are:

- The throwing of objects that can cause even slight injury towards the sport field or against any other person.
- The assault against others, regardless of the fact that there may be no body damages, as well as the threatening against any person among those whose name is written in the score sheet.
- The possession and the use of objects that may cause body damage.
- The disposition of fireworks, firecrackers and other flammable materials.
- The entrance to sports facilities with a covered face to avoid being recognized.

309. All these acts are punished if they are committed during a sport event within the sport facility or around it or in the parking areas and the areas of arrival of spectators by imprisonment of at least six months and up to five years plus fine. The sentence may under no circumstances be suspended, and the sanctions may not be commuted to fine penalty. The court that issues the condemning decision also imposes on the guilty person the prohibition to attend sport events with the participation of his/her team for a period no less than six months and no longer than two years starting after the execution of the main sanction. During this period, the condemned person has an obligation to appear at the closest to his residence police station and stay there from the beginning until the end of every match in which his/her team participates. Certain provisions for the fast procedure of the trial in such cases are also included in the law.

310. In paragraphs 2 and 2A of Article 41ST, some other actions are included of the sport violence crime, such as:

- The entrance in the main area of the sport field or in the teams and referees' dressing rooms of anybody that is not entitled to by the regulations of the relevant federation before, during or after a match with the purpose to disturb its performance or to cause violent incident commits any of the crimes of paragraph 1.

- To commit any of the actions of the main crime of paragraph 1 because of a sport event, before or after it, even away from the sport facility. Due to its vague content, it is necessary to further define the place of this crime in a more specific way, such as in the areas where the fans of the participating teams gather and pass on their way to the sport facility.
- To address against any other person racist expressions or expressions insulting his/her nationality, the national anthem or the Olympic symbols.

311. These actions are punished with imprisonment of three months to five years plus fine. The sentence may under no circumstances be suspended, and the sanctions may not be commuted to fine penalty. The court that issues the condemning decision also imposes on the guilty person the prohibition to attend sport events with the participation of his/her team as described above.

312. In paragraph 3, it is set that in case the perpetrator of one of the above actions seems by the way he acted to be extremely dangerous for the normal operation of sport events, the imposed imprisonment may be at least two years and up to five years. The perpetrator may be considered extremely dangerous, especially when he has committed in the past similar crimes or participated in violent incidents playing a basic role or acted according to a plan or caused severe damages.

313. In all the above crimes, it is foreseen that if the perpetrator commits the same action in another more serious crime, such as murder, which is punished more severely by the PC or other penal laws, he is only punished for the more serious crime.

314. Apart from those crimes set out in paragraphs 1–3, there are twenty more crimes defined in paragraph 4 of the same Article. As far as these crimes are concerned, it should be noted that they are also set out as simple crimes in the PC, with the only difference that once these crimes occur in a sport field or in relation to a sport activity under the circumstances of the paragraphs 1 and 2, the penalties are stricter. The additional sanction of prohibition to attend sport events, the prohibition of suspension as well as the other regulations of legal procedure included in this article also apply.

315. The crimes foreseen in paragraph 4 are the disturbance of the public peace and order, the provocation or praise of a felony, the insults against religions, the obstruction of transports, the body damage, the clash, the illegal violence, the threat, the disturbance of house peace and order, the offence against the sexual dignity, the cause of a scandal with indecent acts and the blackmail.

D. Administrative and Disciplinary Sanctions

316. Finally, in Article 41Z of law 2725/1999, as introduced by law 3057/2002 and amended several times so far, administrative sanctions and the minimum disciplinary sanctions to be imposed according to the federations' regulations are set. The federations may include in their regulations and apply the sanctions foreseen in the law or more severe sanctions.

317. An example of an administrative measure is the prohibition of the distribution of tickets to any sport association's fan club (paragraph 2), the revocation of the special sports recognition by the General Secretariat of Sport to any sport association (paragraph 9) or the reduction or the suspension of the allocations from the State to any sport federation (paragraph 10) that violates the provisions of the law. Article 1 of law 4326/2015 introduced another administrative measure giving the right to the Deputy Minister of Sport to impose fines from EUR 10,000 up to EUR 1,000,000 to associations, TAA, AAE or even sport federations or professional leagues in case of serious violent incidents related to sport (paragraph 2). The Minister may also impose a fine of EUR 5,000 up to EUR 500,000 in case of provocation of violence through media or web (paragraph 5). He may also decide to temporarily or definitely stop the championship or not allow certain matches to take place, having the right to impose fines of EUR 25,000 up to EUR 5,000,000 in case of breach of his decision (paragraph 3). He may also impose fines of EUR 5,000 up to EUR 100,000 on associations, TAA, AAE, sport federations or professional leagues for non-collaboration in the investigation of violent incidents (paragraph 4). The above administrative measures may be taken irrespective of any disciplinary decision of the competent judiciary organ of the federation or the league, and the respective decisions may be appealed in the administrative courts.

318. The disciplinary sanctions are inflicted on athletes, coaches, administrative members, sport associations, TAA, AAEs and professional leagues by decision of the competent judicial institution. Some of the sanctions inflicted in this case are:

- For the athletes and coaches, their ban from sport events and matches for at least two matches or the respective period of time plus fine.
- For the members of the Board of Sport Associations, TAA and AAEs, their representatives and those connected with them with a professional relationship, the prohibition of their entrance into sport facilities during sport events and the loss of their position for at least one month plus fine.
- For the sport association, TAA or AAE, a considerable fine as well as the deprivation of the right to have fans in their home matches for at least one match. It is worth mentioning here that the strict liability rule also applies to the sport associations, TAA or AAEs whose fans, athletes, coaches or administrators commit a disciplinary offence of sport violence. According to this, in all these cases, the above actions may apply even without proof of guilt or negligence of the association, TAA or AAE.
- For the professional league, there is a considerable fine.

319. Apart from all these measures and sanctions, there are also some other provisions, the role of which is both preventive and suppressive. These are:

– The deprivation of the sport quality, e.g., the contemporary or permanent ban on watching any sport event or participating in any kind of sport institution (association, union, federation, etc.) either as an athlete or coach or trainer or member of a sport association or doctor, etc. This penalty cannot be considered a disciplinary one since it is not inflicted by any sport judicial institution, but it is imposed by a special committee of the EO, the EFIPID which replaced the EFIP, according to Article 130 of law 2725/1999. This is why this sanction should be considered of an administrative nature. The abovementioned committee can impose this penalty whenever an athlete, a coach, a member of a sport association, etc., is remanded there by the competent judiciary institution of the federation he belongs to.
– The revocation of the professional licence of a coach according to Article 31, paragraph 7 of law 2725/1999. This administrative sanction is imposed with a decision of the Minister of Sport, after the proposal of the sport federation the coach belongs to.
– Prohibition for those who have been irrevocably sentenced for acts of sport violence to become members of sport association, boards of administration and committees of unions, federations, fan clubs, referees' associations, etc., or even to acquire the licence to exercise the duties of a coach. These administrative sanctions are set out in Article 3, paragraph 1b of law 2725/1999.

IV. Bribery – Match Fixing

320. While violence has been a long-lasting problem in sport and doping exploded at the end of the previous century, match fixing has undoubtedly become the major issue sports internationally face as a challenge in the current century. In Greece, it has been considered a serious crime since 1975 to bribe for the alteration of the result of a match. It is true though that today, with the invasion of bets in the life of the majority of sport fans, the way it takes place has seriously changed, since instead of offering and receiving money aiming at the alteration of a sport result, people involved prefer to have the expected profit through betting not only in the final result of a match but also in many other facts of a match to which betting is nowadays possible, such as result of the first half, possibility of penalty, number of corner kicks or yellow cards.

321. It is self-evident that the crime of bribery with the aim of altering in an unfair way a match result constitutes a very serious sport crime. Match fixing harms not only the sport ideal, the Olympic Ideals, and fair play but also the sport teams as organized companies, the athletes and even the sports fans who bet on sport activities. It falsifies the result of a match and the sport competition itself. In the history of Greek football championships in the seventies, some serious bribery cases were revealed and sanctioned. In the years that followed, suspicions of other bribery cases which were never revealed harmed the reliability of those competitions. In the last decade, criminal authorities investigated at least three huge cases with the involvement of many persons participating in sports activity, but the majority of them were not condemned.

322. The crime of bribery is set out in Article 132 of law 2725/1999, as it has been replaced with Article 13 of law 4049/2012, its passive form (reception of money, gifts or promises) in paragraph 2, its active form (giving or money, gifts or promises) in paragraphs 1 and 3 and its distinguished form (when the alteration of the game result is proved to have been achieved) in paragraph 4.

323. The crime of bribery in its passive form can be committed by anybody who requests, accepts or receives money, gifts, benefits or other grants or promises for money, gifts, benefits or other grants in order to falsify the result of a match. Though, the ones who are logically able to commit such a crime are the athletes, the referees, and administrative members of the teams and people connected to all the above, such as their wives/husbands, parents or friends.

324. On the contrary, the crime of bribery in its active form can literally be committed by anybody, who could be someone who has a special interest in the result of a match because he is the proprietor, administrative member, coach, athlete, etc., of a team or even a sport fun who expects to get profit from bet through an unexpected match result. The act of this crime is to either intervene with unfair actions in order to influence the progression or the result of a match of any team or individual sport (paragraph 1) or give or promise money, gifts, benefits or other grants to athletes, referees and administrative members of the teams and people connected to them or to an association, an AAE or a TAA (paragraph 2).

325. This crime can be committed either before or during a sport event. The penalty for this crime as set out in Article 132 of law 2725/1999, is imprisonment of one year to five years plus fine of at least EUR 100,000 up to EUR 500,000 for the intervention of paragraph 1 and imprisonment of two years to five years plus fine of at least EUR 200,000 up to EUR 1,000,000 for offering or receiving money, gifts, benefits or other grants according to paragraphs 2 and 3.

326. In paragraph 4 of Article 132, there is a special provision for an even stricter penalty of imprisonment for at least five years up to ten years once the alteration of a match result is proved to have been achieved.

327. Paragraph 5 of this article contains a provision that if any of the persons involved in such actions make possible by announcement to the authorities the prevention of a crime of bribery or contribute to the punishment of involved persons, they may be released or receive a smaller sanction.

328. Regarding match-fixing, it is necessary to add that Greece has signed the European Convention on the Manipulation of Sports Competitions of 18 September 2014 (Magglingen/Macolin Convention) which is ratified by law 4639/2019.

329. Needless to say, bribery also constitutes a very serious disciplinary offence severely punished both by the judicial institutions of the relevant sport unions or federations, which organize the competition where bribery took place and by EFIPID with the deprivation of sport quality from the persons involved even for life.

V. Other Genuine Sport Crimes

330. The arbitrary giving of an allocation for a purpose other than what it was granted for is standardized in Article 50, paragraph 5 of law 2725/1999. The objective of this provision is to ensure that the allocations given from the General Secretariat of Sport, which is the public institution competent for the protection and reinforcement of the sport activity, are used for the purpose they were given.

331. The abovementioned crime can be committed by a member of the administration, by an employee of any institution that receives financial aid from the General Secretariat of Sport, or by any other person who deals with money allocated from the General Secretariat of Sport.

332. The institutions that receive money from the General Secretariat of Sport are the sport associations, the sport unions, the sport federations, the HOC, the sport association and federation for the disabled, the coaches' associations, the referees' associations, the major events organizing committees, the national gymnasiums and sport centres, local authorities, etc. In the past, TAA, AAEs and the professional leagues of football and basketball were not receiving allocations from the State, but this has changed lately because they are entitled to receive allocations as part of the profit of the State from the taxation of the betting companies.

333. The allocations granted to these institutions may serve different goals, such as the execution of programs for the development of a certain sport activity, the confrontation of their functional needs, the coverage of the expenses for their participation in sport events, the construction, maintenance and improvement of sport facilities, etc.

334. The penalty for this crime varies from imprisonment of ten days up to two years plus fine and in severe cases depending on the total amount of money used for a purpose other than it was granted for and on whether this criminal behaviour resulted in illegal profit higher than EUR 15,000 the penalty is imprisonment of two to five years and if it exceeds EUR 60,000 or lasted long imprisonment for up to twenty years.

335. The law, in an attempt to strictly control the function of the professional leagues, the TAA and the AAEs through the EEA, wishes to make sure that its members can have access to any book, account or document they think is necessary for their work. This is the reason the legislator has made a special provision in Article 77A, paragraph 2 of law 2725/1999, setting out the crime of the refusal to give information or documents to the EEA. This crime can be committed by any member of a TAA, an AAE or a professional league and is sanctioned with imprisonment of ten days up to three years or a fine.

336. The law recently contains a new similar provision in Article 52A that anyone connected in any way with the sport institution controlled by the General Inspector of Public Administration who denies or delays in providing evidence in his possession that has been asked or provides false or inaccurate evidence is sanctioned with imprisonment of at least two to five years and fine of EUR 100,000.

337. The law in Articles 61 and 69 has set several limitations for those who wish to undertake the administration of a TAA or buy shares or undertake the management of an AAE. For example, it is in principle prohibited among others to athletes, coaches, referees and players or coaches' agents as well to those having shares or the management of another AAE of the same sport and their wives/husbands and close relatives to buy shares or undertake the management of AAEs. Apart from the invalidity of these transactions, the guilty person may be condemned to imprisonment from ten days to five years and a fine of up to EUR 500,000.

VI. Body Damages: Penal Provisions and Tort Law

A. *Introduction*

338. The most common of the non-genuine sport crimes is that of body damage, which is set out in Articles 308–315 of the PC.[14] Body damage may in severe cases result in death, as set out in Article 311 of the PC. In this case, the action may also be considered as homicide (Articles 299–302 PC). No special reference will be made in the following paragraphs for those cases, since their confrontation regarding the issues under examination in principle is not different from the confrontation of body damages.

339. It is commonplace that sport activity is subject to the rules and the provisions of the common penal and civil law. In Greece, just as in most European countries, there is no special legislation for the penal and civil liability from the exercise of a sport activity. Therefore, the common and general provisions of the civil and penal law are applied whenever a matter of penal or civil liability arises during a sport activity. Provided the fact that body damages (especially among the athletes) are often the case during a sport event, the main issue that must be examined is to what extent the civil and, in particular, the penal law falls back in front of the rules of the sport legal order.

340. It would be really irrational if the State, which proclaims that it wants to protect sport and to support the sport activity by promoting sports such as boxing or football, intervened and punished a boxer who following the rules of the game, punches his opponent, or a football player, who, by committing a foul, causes damage to a member of the rival team.

341. On the contrary, it would also be irrational and dangerous if the sport activity remained out of any penal or civil control and limit. In this case, there would be a place of penal and civil immunity, e.g., a situation that cannot be accepted by any organized society.

14. Elements are taken from the work of A. Mavromatis, *Penal Crimes in Sport*, 2002, 257, etc.

B. Body Damages Related to Sport Activity

342. The body damages appearing before or during a sport activity, or even because of it, can be classified into various categories, dependent on the victim and the reason that caused them.

a. Body Damages to Athletes Directly Connected to Their Exercising Sport Activity

a1. Body Damage Due to Bad Training

343. If the athlete's injury is the result of his executing the exercise badly, whether during the training or during the match, he is liable for the damage he has caused to himself since self-injury is not, in principle, punishable by Greek law.

344. On the contrary, if the athlete's injury is put down to the fact that he attempted to carry out an exercise for which he was not properly prepared, either because he is a beginner or because he is still in the first stages of his preparation or due to the excessive frequency of his training or because he had to confront an opponent much more experienced or stronger than him, then his coach may be responsible for his injury.

345. Of course, it is rare that the coach deliberately causes damage to the athlete he has to supervise. Usually, the coach causes such damage to the athlete because of his negligence. When the case is so, his penal and civil liability will be found in the general provisions of the Penal and the CC.

346. The coach's special legal obligation results from the work contract he has signed with a sport association, union, or AAE. Because of this contract and because of his specialized scientific knowledge, a coach has the special obligation to comply with some rules, the omission of which constitutes the crime of the body damage from negligence. Some of these rules are:

- the giving of instructions for the rules of performance and safety of a sport activity, the possible dangers and the right way to perform the training and the match;
- the preparation of the athlete and the supervision of his right training;
- the approval of an athlete's participation in a match and his supervision during it.

a2. Body Damage Due to Late Diagnosis or Delayed and Inappropriate Medical Help

347. There is no need to argue about the necessity of medical surveillance on athletes, taking into consideration the fact that they exercise daily in a strenuous way, especially when they are athletes of a high level. So, in case the athlete undergoes damage because of an already existent problem which the doctor failed to detect, or because of a wrong supply of medical help, the doctor may be liable out of negligence for the damage caused to the athlete.

348. In general, the lack of caution on the part of the doctor is the result of his violating one of the following obligations:

- preventive medical examination of the athlete before any sport activity;
- surveillance of the training and the matches and giving first aid to athletes undergoing body injuries during the sport activity;
- indication of the proper therapeutic treatment to athletes suffering from injuries and certification of their readiness to return to their training and matches.

Apart from the doctor, an administrative member of the team may also be liable for injuries if he/she fails to fulfil his/her obligation to have the athletes of the team examined by a doctor. This obligation is set out in Article 33, paragraph 9 of law 2725/1999.

349. Subject to the same liability may be the referee of the game as well, in case he has not forbidden, as he is obliged to according to Article 33, paragraph 9 of law 2725/1999, the participation in the game of an athlete who is not equipped with a certification that he is healthy.

a3. Body Damage Due to Non-use or Bad Use of the Equipment (Suit, Knee-Caps, Association, Gloves, Racket, Etc.)

350. In many sports, the athlete must carry special equipment apart from his sport uniform. It is very often the case that the athlete gets hurt due to lack of the necessary equipment or because of the bad use of it. In these cases, liable for his injuries may be: (a) his coach, especially when the athlete is young or inexperienced, and his coach did not indicate to him the necessity of the use or the proper use of the equipment, (b) an administrative member of the team, responsible for the materials and the equipment of the athletes, or even responsible for their proper maintenance, (c) the head referee, if he allowed, contrary to the rules, to an athlete to carry an equipment able to cause injuries, or, on the contrary, if he allowed the participation of an athlete in the game without the proper equipment, and (d) the manufacturer, the seller or the one who is responsible for maintaining the equipment.

a4. Body Damage Due to Imperfections of the Sport Field or Due to Bad Weather Conditions

351. In the sports of sheltered and open fields, the sport facilities must be in good condition according to the rules of each sport so that the injuries of the participants are avoided. This obligation usually belongs to the competence of the manufacturer and the owner of the sport facilities, the organizer of the sport event and the referee of the sport meeting.

352. The manufacturer is obliged to hand in the sport field to the owner in good condition, absolutely safe for the organization of a sport event, according to the special rules of each sport.

353. The owner of a sport facility, e.g., the sport association, TAA or the AAE which allows its use to its athletes, or any other person or institution of public or private law that hires it for a sport association, TAA or limited company has to take all the measures set out in the law in order to keep the sport facilities in good condition.

354. The organizer of the sport event, who has rent the facilities from the owner, has the obligation to make sure that the sport field is in the proper condition before the beginning of the sport event.

355. The head referee must also check the condition of the sport field before any sport meeting. This obligation of his is usually set out within the special regulations of each sport.

356. In case the abovementioned people or legal entities do not comply with their obligations, then they may be judged guilty of the crime of body injury from negligence.

a5. Body Damage Due to Touch, Collision or Attack of the Opponent Athlete

357. Among all the body injuries an athlete may undergo during a sport event, the most usual and the most controversial one is the one caused by touch, collision or attack of another athlete. Although in this case there may be a disciplinary liability of the athlete, the crucial issue is whether there is also a penal and tortuous liability.

The answer to this question depends on two factors. The first is the kind of sport in which the touch, the collision or even the attack took place. The second one is the kind of theory we adopt and choose in order to minimize the athlete's penal and tortuous liability.

358. With regard to the kind of sport activity a touch, collision or attack happens in, sports are divided into the following categories:

- sports of allowed violence or armed collision (e.g., wrestling, boxing, judo, fencing, etc.);
- sports of body touch (football, basketball, water polo, softball, etc.);
- sports without any contact among the athletes (racing, swimming, volleyball, tennis, etc.).

359. In Greece, both theory and jurisprudence agree that in most cases of injuries happening even against each sport's special regulations but within a normal acceptable framework for each sport, the athletes should not be subject to any penal liability. Supporters of this opinion invoke different theories to ground it:

- theory of the victim's consent;
- theory of the prevailing custom;
- theory of the lack of fraud;

- theory of the recognition of the sport goal from the State;
- theory of the exercise of a right;
- theory of the lack of threat against the society;
- theory of the social benefits of the sport activity;
- theory of a generally accepted jeopardy;
- theory of the acceptance of jeopardy;
- theory of the risky life of the legal goods.

360. This conclusion, that there should not be any penal liability of the responsible athlete, stands for all injuries resulting from actions not prohibited by the relevant sport regulation (i.e., an acceptable by the rules punch in a boxing match) in all sport categories as well as for injuries resulting from usual light violations of the regulations in sports of body touch (i.e., a foul committed by a football player usual in football matches).

361. On the contrary, if the injury results from a non-usual against the spirit of the sport violation of the regulations in sports of body touch (i.e., when the defender attacks his opponent with a hit karate style) or from any violation of the regulations both in sports of allowed violence (i.e., a prohibited punch at the back of the head in boxing, since it may be extremely risky for the opponent's health, even for his life) and in sports without contact between the athletes (i.e., when a swimmer hits one of his competitors, since it is absolutely against the spirit of this sport), the athlete that caused it has full penal responsibility.

362. It is worth mentioning though that in some cases of body damage due to the touch, collision or attack by the opponent, there may be other persons responsible for the body damage who acting against the regulations or the law allowed this to happen. These persons may be: (a) the referee, i.e., for not interrupting a boxing game where one boxer was attacking against the regulations, (b) the doctor of the game, i.e., for allowing an injured athlete to continue, (c) the organizer of a sport event, i.e., for organizing a game in a sport of allowed violence against the regulations that divide athletes into categories according to their age, weight and experience between a young, small or completely inexperienced athlete and an older, bigger and stronger, resulting in the injury of the first one, (d) the administrative member of an association for allowing athletes of the association to participate in games such the one described above, and (e) the coaches for similar reasons.

a6. Body Damage Due to Use of Forbidden Substances or Methods Given to the Athlete or Used by Him in Order to Improve His Performance and Efficiency

363. As described, lower doping is risky for the athletes' health. It is obvious that if body damage occurs to an athlete because of the use of a prohibited substance or a prohibited method, the person who administered this substance or method to him/her (coach, doctor, physiotherapist, administrative member or even just a friend, etc.) has full penal responsibility for the body damage in addition to his/her responsibility for the doping crime he/she committed. The only difficulty is that since in most of the cases the body damage caused by doping can only be discovered after a long time, it is often difficult to prove the exact reason for it and who was the responsible person who administered it.

b. Body Damages of Athletes, Referees, Coaches, Administrative Members and Other People Taking Part in a Sport Activity or of Spectators Indirectly Connected to It

b1. Body Damage During the Sport Activity and Because of It

364. During the sport activity, especially in some sports where dangerous equipment is used (i.e., javelin or hammer in track and fields) or the equipment is used in a way that becomes dangerous (i.e., a ball can be hit extremely strongly) or even the sports are dangerous by nature due to speed (i.e., car races), it is possible that injuries may be caused because of the sport activity. Such cases are, for example, injuries because of a strong kick of the ball in football, because of an athlete's fall on a photographer in basketball, because of a mistaken throwing of the hammer, or because of an overturning of a race car.

365. In these cases, the athletes are not the victims as in all the previous categories, but the responsible persons for the body damages. In most of the above cases, there should not be any penal liability of the responsible athlete because these injuries result either from actions not prohibited by the relevant sport regulation or from usual light violations of the regulation. The only case where the athlete should have penal responsibility is when he/she acted on purpose (i.e., threw the javelin to the spectators) or showed inexcusable negligence (i.e., started his effort in the hammer throw without the existence of the protecting net).

b2. Body Damage Due to Lack of Security Measures from the Organizers of a Sport Event or Due to Lack of Safety of the Sport Facilities

366. In order to avoid accidents like the ones described above, in all sport regulations there are some provisions for the security of all involved persons (athletes, referees, coaches, administrative members, spectators, etc.). The organizer of any sport event has the obligation to follow all the security requirements foreseen in the regulation. If he/she fails to do so and an incident takes place resulting in the injury of any person related to the sport activity, he/she has full penal responsibility. Such security measures are also those referring to the normal arrival and departure of the spectators in the sport facility and all those decided by the competent authorities in order to avoid violent incidents. Greece faced a very serious accident in 1981 when about thirty people died in a football match Olympiakos – AEK in Stadium Karaiskaki, trying to exit from the stadium while the doors were still closed.

367. The organizers of the sport events as well as the constructors and the owners of the sport facilities, also face another kind of possible penal responsibility, if they violate the rules and the scientific data for the construction or the maintenance of sport facilities, the number of spectators that should be allowed to stay in the tiers, etc.

368. Regarding safety and security in sports events, Greece has signed the European Convention of 3 July 2016 for integrated security, protection and access to services in football matches and other sports events, but it has not yet been ratified by law. Until then, various provisions of laws other than sports law are applied, especially in football; UEFA regulations to prevent safety and security issues,[15] together with the regulations of the HFF (EPO).

b3. Body Damage Due to Assault Committed by a Spectator, an Athlete, a Referee, a Coach, Etc.

369. As described above, violence in sport may result in the injury of the involved persons. It is obvious that if body damage occurs to a spectator, an athlete, a coach, a referee or anybody involved in the event because of the assault, the responsible person has full penal responsibility for the body damage in addition to his/her responsibility for the crime of violence in sport he/she committed.

C. Penal and Tortuous Liability of Legal Entities

370. Greek legal system does not recognize the application of strict liability in criminal law nor criminal responsibility of legal persons. Therefore, in criminal law, liability lies with the natural person who committed the action or the omission. Criminal liability of an administrator of a legal person can be established only if the crime may be attributed to him as a failure to comply with the obligations set by rules or regulations.

371. It is reasonable that in all cases of an athlete's injury, apart from the criminal liability of the one who caused it, there is also the matter of his disciplinary liability, according to the rules of the respective sport, which is administered by the competent disciplinary institution of each sport union, federation or league, and the matter of his tortuous liability (*see* next chapter), which is set out in the relative provisions of the Greek Civil Code (Articles 914 et seq. CC). According to Article 914, whoever damages another illegally and culpably has an obligation to compensate him.

372. As far as the right to bring an action in civil courts for remuneration is concerned, this must be recognized to the athlete who has suffered from the body injury, otherwise the victim of the tort. The same applies in case the victim of the injury is any other person related to the sport activity.

373. There is a question though, whether this action can be brought to courts by the legal entity (association, TAA, limited company, etc.) the athlete belongs to. According to Article 914 of the Greek Civil Code, in combination with Article 63 of the Code of Penal Procedure, this right is recognized only to a person who has

15. Football has faced internationally the most serious security incidents related to sports events with several people having lost their lives because of them, such as the incidents in Heysel in the European Champion's Cup 1985, the Hillsborough disaster 1989, etc.

directly and immediately suffered from the crime or the tort. This is why the right to bring an action is only accepted for the athlete-victim and not for the legal entity he/she is part of.

374. A further issue that must be examined is who is responsible for compensating for an injury caused to an athlete; in other words, who the action must be brought against in case of an injury caused by another athlete. Beyond the athlete-victimizer, who caused the damage, liable to remunerate the athlete-victim is also the legal entity the athlete-victimizer belongs to, on condition that he/she is a professional or at least a paid athlete, connected to his/her legal entity with a working contract. In this case, the legal entity is responsible for its athletes and for the torts committed by them (vicarious liability) according to Article 922 of the CC. Nevertheless, if the athlete is just an amateur, his/her association possesses no liability for his illegal behaviour.

375. Article 922 of the CC contains a provision that in case the victimizer is a natural person acting in the frame of his duties as employee or administrator, then the claim may also be brought against the legal person who is co-responsible to pay the damages to the victim. This principle applies to all body damages related to sport as described above.

VII. Civil Sports Liability

376. Sports civil liability (responsabilité civile sportive) is civil liability for damages caused during the conduct of sports competitions and sports activities in general or in the context of sports competitions and sports activities in general and which constitute in concreto a violation of the right to health and physical integrity or even in the lives of athletes, fans and other persons.

In particular, in the context of the expanded concept of illegal, sports civil liability is also accepted in concreto in the event of an omission that constitutes a breach of the obligations of care, welfare, safety and protection, i.e., in the event that sports organizations do not take the necessary and necessary measures, including those that may have been indicated by the relevant Police Authority (Article 41D, paragraph 1 Law 2725/1999), to ensure fully safe sports facilities and conditions for sports competitions and sports activities in general (e.g., on the road in the case of cycling, at sea in the case of sailing, rowing, canoeing, kayaking and water skiing, etc.) and to prevent the risk of infringement of the right to health and physical integrity or even in the lives of athletes, fans and other persons. In fact, this security obligation is increased (obligation de sécurité renforcée) in case of dangerous sports, e.g., motorcycle, motorsports, skiing, climbing, etc.

According to Articles 297, 298, 914 and 932 of the CC, conditions for the civil liability of private individuals (natural persons and legal entities under private law) for compensation or monetary satisfaction for moral damage caused by tort are the illegal behaviour of the person liable for compensation towards the person who was damaged, the culpability of the obligee, which exists in the case of fraud and negligence, that is, when the diligence required in transactions is not paid, the existence of damage and the existence of a causal connection between the illegal conduct and the damage.

The illegal conduct, as a condition of the tort, can consist not only of a positive act in the sense of violating the general duty imposed by the provision of Article 914 of the CC not to harm someone else culpably, but also an omission, as long as in this last case, the one who fell into the omission was obliged to act by the law or legal action or by good faith and commercial and good morals according to the prevailing social concept. Therefore, illegal conduct as a prerequisite exists in all actions or omissions described above, leading to body injuries related to sports if the victimizer is considered criminally liable. In the event that someone creates a dangerous situation from which damage could result to others, the principle of good faith imposes the appropriate positive action to avoid causing damage to third parties from this situation.

In view of these, it has been accepted in the context of private law that sports civil liability of individuals is established by omission in the following cases:

- in the event that a sports program organizer in a swimming pool (swimming pool) and additional safety supervisors fail to guide the athletes to a swimming pool intended for their age and to intervene in a timely manner with support personnel to restore an aspiration emergency caused by swimming in an unsuitable swimming pool, resulting in causation of brain damage and neurological problems in an athlete who remains in the water for a considerable period of time from suction;
- in the event that an organizer of a boxing sports match fails to organize a match in a sports facility with a surface suitable for this sport and capable of absorbing the shocks from a strong fall of an athlete, resulting in a causative injury to an athlete who falls on this surface;
- in the event that a sports gymnastics club fails to organize training in a sports facility with a surface suitable for this sport and capable of absorbing the shocks of a strong fall of an athlete, resulting in a causative injury to an athlete who falls on this surface;
- in the event that a wrestling sports association fails to ensure that wrestling training is divided into categories with athletes of similar size, weight, technique and experience, resulting in a causative injury to a smaller and less experienced athlete training with a larger athlete and more experience;
- in the event that the organizer of an athletics event fails to create a special finishing corridor after the finish line, which ensures sufficient space for reducing speed and stopping in a safe manner, resulting in a causally related injury to an athlete who collides with an obstacle located a few meters after the finish line;
- in the event that a 5×5 soccer field management and operator fails to mark a dangerous point with wire mesh on the corridor for the transition from the box office located at the entrance to the field, resulting in a causative injury to an athlete who bumps into this wire mesh;
- in the event that an organizer of a motorcycle sports race fails to mark the dangerous points on the borders of the track (e.g., trees or other obstacles), which

could lead to injury to the competing athletes, resulting in a causative injury to an athlete who passes through these points;
- in the event that the home team of a football match fails to distribute the fans of the two opposing teams evenly and smoothly within the sports facility, to prevent the throwing of flares and pieces of cement by its fans and to prevent overcrowding and compression of the away team's fans team in a confined space to avoid flares and chunks of cement, resulting in causative injury to an away team fan from a falling horizontal guardrail;
- in the event that the home team of a football match and an additional private company providing security services (Article 41D, paragraph 11a of Law 2725/1999) fail to carry out a thorough check of incoming fans for any dangerous objects, resulting in a causal relevance injury to a police officer or a fan from dangerous objects that pass the control and are used against him.

Regarding the civil liability of the legal persons it is worth mentioning that it also stands for the State, OTA and legal entities of public law. According to Articles 105–106 of Introductory Law of the CC, conditions for civil liability of the State, OTA and legal entities of public law for compensation or monetary satisfaction for moral damage from tort is the illegal behaviour of the person liable for compensation towards the one who was damaged, which was in the exercise of public authority, the existence of damage and the existence of a causal link between the illegal conduct and the damage. Civil liability of the State also arises from non-legal material actions of the State bodies, OTAs and legal entities under public law or from omissions due to legal material actions thereof, as long as these material actions or omissions are related to the organization and operation of public services. In addition, there is the responsibility of the State, local authorities and legal entities under public law, subject to the other conditions of the law, not only when a specific provision of the law is violated by an act or omission of an organ, but also when the special duties and obligations assigned to the specific service are omitted and are determined by the existing general legislation, the lessons of common experience and the principles of good faith. In view of these, it has also been accepted in the context of public law that sports civil liability of the State, local authorities and legal entities of public law is established. For example:

- in the event that the bodies of the Greek Police, which are responsible for ensuring public peace and order and the smooth social life of citizens and maintaining order during sports meetings inside and outside the competition venues (Article 8 of Law 2800/2000 and Article 41D of Law 2725/1999), fail to intervene with the aim of taking protective measures in favour of citizens and their properties before, during and after the end of sports competitions, both inside and outside the competition grounds, with the result that causation injury from the situations created;
- in the event that a management and operator of a municipal football sports facility fails to take the necessary safety measures and to mark a dangerous point due to work being carried out, as a result of which an injury to a spectator who fell at the work site is causally caused.

VIII. Gambling – Sports Betting

377. Greece decided to permit online gambling, for the first time, by Law 4002/ 2011, while local Internet users were already offered such services contrary to the pre-existing prohibition. The law of 2011 introduced a licensing system on the basis of public tenders. Despite the provision made by lawmakers, no such public tender ever took place. Instead, online gambling was temporarily authorized on the basis of a transitory regime introduced by the same law of 2011. This regime allowed operators licensed at that time in any country of the European Economic Area (EEA) to continue offering their services in Greece if they would voluntarily become (by the end of 2011) subject to retroactive taxation of their past profits (as of 2010). A total of twenty-four whitelisted operators were thereby allowed to offer online gambling activities in Greece.

A. *Hellenic Gaming Commission*

378. In 2011, the Hellenic Gaming Commission (HGC) was created to be the country's independent administrative authority when it comes to the rules and regulations under which all gaming and gambling services must operate in Greece, which happens through supervision, monitoring and rule of law. HGC has nine members directly appointed by the Minister of Finance. The terms and conditions for applying for a licence in Greece are defined by HGC in Law 4002/2011.

The HGC adopted a set of general principles which govern its activities relating to its operation and the execution of its regulatory functions:

(a) Proportionality: The HGC must only intervene if necessary. All measures adopted must be appropriate to prevent the risk they address, and all costs they entail for the regulated entity must be justified.
(b) Accountability: The HGC must justify its decisions and be subject to public scrutiny.
(c) Consistency: The HGC must lay down regulatory frameworks whose provisions and requirements are consistent with each other and demonstrate impartiality in their enforcement.
(d) Transparency: The HGC must be honest, establish simple and clear regulatory frameworks and formulate them in such a way as to be easily understood by the users.
(e) Commitment: The HGC must be committed to resolving problems and minimize the negative impact that its decisions are likely to have.
(f) Social responsibility and empathy: In order to ensure responsible gaming, the HGC must be aware of and familiar with the needs of the public at large and be in direct and open contact with the citizens, focusing primarily on vulnerable groups.

The regulatory tasks of the HGC consist of a series of Regulations that apply either to the gaming market as a whole (horizontal) or to specific games or game categories, or, finally, to the operation and the operators of such games.

After the 2011 Gambling Act was adopted, foreign operators could apply for a licence, but few were willing to invest because of the lack of clarity around licensing procedures, plus the government tax rate of 30%, which only applies to non-domestic companies. This led to the country being sued and in 2013, the EU ruled the OPAP monopoly was illegal which led to the Greek government selling off a one-third stake in OPAP to private investors.

Finally, after years of procrastination, Greece overhauled the licensing system concerning online gambling by Law 4635/2019 which amended the provisions of Law 4002/2011. The law of 2019 departs from the rationale of public tenders (never implemented in practice) and allows any interested parties to obtain fixed-term renewable licences for the provision of online gambling. The new framework has been complemented by a series of regulatory decisions issued by the Minister of Financial Affairs in August 2020.

Considering these developments, on 11 September 2020, the HGC issued a public invitation to apply for online gambling licences. This is an open-ended process accessible not only to prospective new entrants but also to the operators under the hitherto transitory regime. The latter are eventually obliged to cease business if they fail to apply in a timely manner and obtain a licence.

There are two types of licences that interested parties may apply for: a licence for online betting (Type 1) and a licence for other online games of chance (Type 2).

Type 1 licence has a renewable term of seven years and covers any kind of real events, fantasy sports, virtual events on the basis of a random number generator (RNG), and other events which lend themselves to betting. In order to obtain a Type 1 licence, applicants must, among other conditions, pay fees of EUR 3 million. The same amount is due in respect of a licence renewal.

Type 2 licence has a renewable term of seven years and covers casino games as well as poker and its variants, both if they are played with the help of a dealer (live) without an RNG and if they are based on an RNG. Furthermore, it covers poker and its variants whether carried out on a peer-to-peer basis or as poker cash games or as poker tournaments. In order to obtain a Type 2 licence, applicants must, among other conditions, pay fees of EUR 2 million. The same amount is due in respect of a licence renewal.

B. Fourth Anti-money Laundering Directive

379. Under the 4th Anti-Money Laundering Directive, all providers of gambling services are obliged entities; however, Member States may decide to grant full or partial exemptions to providers of gambling services other than casinos on the basis of proven low risk. Certain gambling products are considered significantly exposed to money laundering risk. In the case of land-based betting and poker, this appears to be due to ineffective controls. For online gambling, there is a high-risk exposure due to very large numbers of transaction flows and the lack of face-to-face interaction. Although casinos present inherently high-risk exposure, their inclusion in the anti-money laundering/countering the financing of terrorism framework since 2005 has had a mitigating effect. Lotteries and gaming machines (outside casinos) present a moderate level of money laundering/terrorist financing risk. For the former, certain controls are in place, in particular, to address the risks associated with high winnings. Land-based bingo is seen as presenting a low level of money laundering/terrorist financing risk due to the relatively low stakes and winnings involved.

Regardless of the policy options finally made, the new framework lays the foundation for a solid online gambling market in Greece and seems to ensure effective supervisory oversight which was lacking under the fragmentary approach of the transitory regime.

§4. Tax

380. As in almost all states in the world and especially in Europe, taxation constitutes the major source of income for the State. Greece used to have an ineffective taxation system in the past, and this along with other parameters led to the lack of sources and the financial crisis of the last decade. Today, the taxation system in Greece has become much more effective, although it should be considered quite heavy for the citizens. Below is a short presentation of the tax system for sporting institutions.[16]

The income of AAEs is considered as profit from business activity. The profit from business activity is determined for each tax year based on the profit and loss account, which is drawn up in accordance with the accounting standards provided for in Greek legislation (total revenue after deducting business expenses). In case the company applies International Accounting Standards, the profit is determined exclusively according to the table of tax results for the year (Articles 21 and 47 of Law 4172/2013).

The profit from the business activity of AAE is taxed at 22% according to Article 58 of Law 4172/2013.

Sports associations, unions and federations, as legal entities of a non-profit nature, are exempt from income tax for all types of income realized in pursuit of their purpose, which are not subject to tax. (Article 45 of Law 4172/2013)

Indicative cases of such income are mentioned, such as contributions (subscriptions) and registration rights of their members, income from fundraisers, government grants, private or business sponsorships, third-party donations, lotteries, from advertisements placed in magazines published and distributed only to their members for free (POL 1044/2015)

The revenues obtained by sports associations, unions or federations from activities that do not constitute the exercise of their non-profit mission are subject to taxation, even if they are allocated to the fulfilment of their non-profit purpose. For example, income from capital (interest, dividends, royalties, income from real estate), from subscriptions from third parties – non-members, income from the publication and sale of magazines, books, forms, etc., to third parties – non-members of the aforementioned persons, as well as from the advertisements registered to them, the income from advertisements on sports club jerseys. (POL 1044/2015)

16. The taxation for employees in sports will be dealt with in Part II (Sport and Employment).

The profit from the business activity of the Sports associations is taxed at 22% according to Article 58 of Law 4172/2013.

§5. Sport Disputes – Sports Justice

381. Under the notion of 'sport dispute', we mean the private or administrative or penal disputes arising in the area of the sport activity, and not a special kind of dispute. The sport disputes can be classified into the following categories:[17]

- Disputes of technical character. These are the disputes arising from the application or the violation of technical rules of a sport, mostly the rules of the game.
- Disputes of administrative character. These are disputes arising from the application or violation of rules of the sport legislation or of the organizing rules of the sport.
- Disputes of disciplinary character. These disputes concern the infliction of disciplinary sanctions resulting from violation of either the rules of the game or the sport legislation.
- Disputes of economic character. These disputes arise from the economic relations among the members of the sport society and concern the infringement of either the common legislation or the regulations of the sport federations.

382. The variety and the special character of the sport disputes force the legislator to define particular public institutions for the settlement of these disputes apart from the common public judging function or to entrust the sport legal entities to establish such institutions, without of course, abandoning the judicial control of the decisions of these institutions. The way and the extension of this control depend on the legal nature of these institutions, the applicable rules and the kind of disputes.

383. Sport justice constitutes a special and very important chapter of the sport legislation, which has to do with the way, the procedure and the instruments of settlement of disputes arising in the sport society and which is occupied with penalties and sanctions imposed for the violation of the rules that govern this particular social area.

384. The Greek legislator uses the term 'sport justice' and makes provisions for instruments and procedures for its dispensation. Sector C of law 2725/1999 had the title 'Sport Justice.' This title has already been modified by law 3057/2002 into 'Disciplinary and Penal Liability.' Chapter A of the abovementioned sector bears the title 'Judging instruments,' which are further divided into First and Second Degree Instruments and ASEAD. Furthermore, Article 128 of law 2725/1999 sets out the notion of the 'Sport Prosecutor', and Article 131 introduces a clause for arbitration for the settlement of purely sport disputes exclusively from the competent sport institutions. The provisions of law 2725/1999 referring to the Sport Justice are found in Articles 95 and 119–132.

17. A. Malatos, *Sport Law Lessons*, 2005, 268.

I. Sport Associations, Unions and Federations and Sports Justice

385. The legal nature of private law of the sport legal entities is set out in Articles 1, 10 and 19 of law 2725/1999. The sport associations, unions and federations are founded and function according to the provisions of the CC and the law 2725/1999.

386. Within the framework of this associational form and nature of the sport legal entities, Articles 5, 14 and 24, paragraph 5 introduce the principle that the statutes of the sport legal entities can arrange a lot of issues concerning their function, among which also the foundation of the instruments that are competent to resolve the sport disputes. Furthermore, Article 27 makes a provision for the issuing of general or special regulations from each sport federation. These regulations put the rules that define the organization and the carrying out of the sport each federation is competent for. When establishing these regulations, international regulations must be taken into account. The observance of these regulations is obligatory for the sport associations and sport unions that fall under the competence of the federation.

387. Moreover, Article 129 defines that 'the relevant sport federations can indicate, with their special regulations, the way, the procedure and the instruments for the settlement of sport disputes, as well as the infliction of disciplinary penalties, for sports or divisions of championships or events for which there is not any particular provision in this law.'

388. According to the abovementioned provisions, the sport federations can establish disciplinary or other instruments for the settlement and resolution of sport disputes that may come up among the participants in their organization and function, or they can even entrust their Board of Administration the exercise of all these tasks.

389. Special provisions for some sports, which the legislator considers to be of high importance for the legal order, are introduced in Articles 119–128 of the sport law. Articles 119 and 120 as amended by laws 3057/2002 and 3262/2004, define that especially for football,[18] basketball, volleyball, handball and water polo, special First-Degree Judicial Instruments are founded in order to execute the tasks set out in Article 120. These tasks are disciplinary (infliction of penalties for the violation of the rules of the game or organizing rules of private or public origin) and administrative (protests against the validity of a match, etc.).

390. It is noteworthy that these special provisions do not concern all the potential disputes in these sports, but only the disputes that are mentioned in Article 119,

18. Football was initially excluded from the provisions of Art. 119, but on 2015 and after long discussion on that issue, with Art. 5 of law 4326/2016 this exclusion was abolished and First Degree Judicial Instruments in football have now the same structure as in other sports. Article 127B though contains still an exception for the First Degree Judicial Instrument of the HFF.

paragraph 2. The other disputes are ruled by the general provisions analysed above. The same happens with the competencies set out in Article 120.

391. With these articles, the law actually adopts a sport justice system of two levels, at least as far as the first degree of settlement is concerned. For the five sports mentioned above, there is a provision for special instruments and competencies, while for the rest of the sports, the sport federations are authorized to define and create the instruments, the competencies and the procedure for the resolution of the sport disputes.

392. The system is unified in the second degree. The institution competent for all sports is ASEAD, which functions as a Second-Degree Judicial Institution. The only exception is for football, where the competent Secondary Judicial Institution is the Appeal Committee of EPO (HFF).

II. The Arbitration Clause

393. With Article 131, paragraph 1, the legislator secures the exclusive competency of the above-described institutions for the settlement of sport disputes, forcing the sport legal entities to include in their statutes a provision 'with which the individuals or the body corporate that take part in the events accept the competence of the arbitrational institutions (set out in the laws or in the regulations) for the resolution of the disputes among them. If such a clause does not exist in the statutes, it is considered to be de jure part of it.'

394. Furthermore, according to Article 131, paragraph 2, the statement of participation in the sport organizations and events constitutes for the participating legal entities a contract of unreserved adhesion to the sport rules of the relevant organization as well as to the correspondent legal provisions and regulations. This statement of participation also binds the athletes, the coaches, etc., even without a special agreement between them and the organizer of the events.

395. With the above provisions, the legislator considers the Institutions of Sport Justice as arbitrational institutions and at the same time makes this characterization compulsory for all the participants in the sport organizations, even if the sport federations have not incorporated a relevant clause in their statutes.

396. Nevertheless, it is worth mentioning here that this exclusive competency of the Sport Judicial Institutions is set out only for the purely sporting disputes and not for all, unexceptionally, the sport disputes. Therefore, according to Article 131, paragraph 1, for purely sporting disputes, the Institutions for the Settlement of Sport Disputes do not function as arbitrational institutions but as instruments of the State or the federations.

397. The above-described legal characterization of sport justice as arbitration is not unquestionably accepted. The approach that this function is of an arbitrational nature is based on the fact that the subjects of the sport activity (athletes, coaches, etc.) accept the competence of the sport judicial institutions as exclusive in order to be entitled to take part in the games. This acceptance may take place either in an explicit way through a written agreement between the athlete and the federation, included in the athlete's registration documents signed by him/her in order to obtain the licence or silently, through the acceptance of the statute of the federation, which happens when the athletes sign registration documents, even if nothing special is mentioned there. In other words, with the signing and the issuing of the licence, the athlete accepts and adheres without any reservations to all the provisions, conditions and clauses of the statute and the regulations of a federation.

398. As far as the associations are concerned, this adhesion takes place through the declaration of participation in any competition by accepting without restriction all the specific rules that govern it, which is necessary for their taking part in the championships. The same adhesion also results from their being members of the federations.

399. In this point, two parameters are worth mentioning, valid for all the institutions of sport justice, even for those that are competent for the settlement of economic disputes, which, as it has already been said, are closer to the model of arbitration.

400. The cornerstone for the replacement of the public judiciary function by the arbitration is the freedom of will of the involved parts to submit their dispute to an arbitrational procedure. Article 8, paragraph 1 of the Greek Constitution prohibits the direct or indirect compulsion to resort to arbitration, even if this compulsion is of legal origin. However, it is more than obvious that an athlete or a sport association willing to participate in a championship or a sport organization has not the freedom to choose his judge (public or private) since the acceptance of the arbitration clause constitutes an obligatory term for his participation. Even if we accept that the arbitration founded on the basis of clauses of the associations' statutes does not involve an inadmissible limitation of its members' free will or of everyone who desires to be part of this association, the existence itself of such kind of clauses and their a priori obligatory acceptance definitely constitutes a limitation of the will of the involved parts to submit their disputes to an arbitration.

401. Furthermore, the elimination of public justice from sport disputes can theoretically be accepted on condition that it does not refer to all the sport disputes but only to those that result from the violation of the playing rules, in other words, to the purely sport disputes. The rest of the sport disputes, or even disputes resulting from the violation of playing rules, involve strict disciplinary sanctions that have a direct impact on somebody's personal rights or life (e.g., a long time elimination due to doping), and the elimination of the public judges appears problematic.

402. It must be mentioned though that as time passes, more and more sports institutions with prominent such as the HFF include in their regulations institutions and regulations for sports dispute resolution, which cover almost all possible disputes, such as for player's registration matters or between their members and this practice seems to be accepted by the associations, athletes, coaches, etc., and silently by the State, which does not react directly, although the more intensive intervention in sports activity as described above, could be considered an indirect reaction.

§6. First-Degree Institutions

403. According to the general provisions of law 2725/1999, within every sport federation there are disciplinary and other judicial institutions, which are established by the federations according to their statutes and regulations on the basis of their private autonomy. The competencies of these institutions can expand to the whole spectrum of the sport justice. Their decisions may be immediately executable, or they may need ratification by the Board of Administration of the federation.

404. Especially for the team sports of football, basketball, volleyball, handball and water polo, the law, due to the major interest of their competitions, especially their highest divisions, has an exceptional provision for the relevant disciplinary institutions. While for the rest of the competitions, the first-degree institutions for the above sports are also established according to their statutory provisions, for the national divisions A1, A2 and B of men and women as well as for the national cup competition, the State itself arranges the establishment of such kind of institutions, according to Article 119 of law 2725/1999. These institutions may not be considered state organs but constitute internal institutions of the respective federations or leagues, although they are established following a compulsory provision of the law

405. These special first-degree judicial institutions in basketball, volleyball, handball and water polo consist of regular, public judges (one plus one reserve per federation) drawn by the Court authorities of the seat of the federation according to the procedure set out in Article 119. Their competencies are set out in Article 120, and they basically concern the infliction of disciplinary sanctions and protests. They may also have some other competencies regarding disputes of technical and administrative nature, which are bestowed to them with legal provisions, regulations and decisions of the sport federations. Article 122 provides the establishment of local first-degree judicial institutions in Thessaloniki competent for disputes arising from matches that take place in the regions of Epirus, Thessaly, Central, Western and Eastern Macedonia and Thrace, but it was never applied.

406. Despite the fact that these institutions function as instruments of the sport federations which also cover their expenses, their difference from the other first-degree institutions described before is that these institutions are founded, organized and work directly due to a legal provision and not as a result of the private autonomy of the sport federations.

407. An even more special provision is set for football. Article 127B of law 2725/1999, as it was added and modified by Article 20, paragraph 4 of law 2947/2001, Article 49 of law 3057/2002 and Article 11 of law 3262/2004, contained a provision for a three-member judicial institution for the professional football which functions within the gulfs of the professional leagues and a three-member disciplinary committee for the amateur football in the federation. Both these institutions should consist according to the law solely of public, regular judges. In practice, the above provision was not followed for many years,[19] and the football authorities had judicial institutions composed of lawyers and ex-judges according to the provision of EPO statutes.

408. In 2015, while Greek football was facing an immense crisis, not only financial, but also with corruption scandals, the Greek State through the Deputy Minister of Sport in collaboration with FIFA and UEFA managed to reach an agreement with the football family for the reorganization of Greek football.[20] One of the first steps was the change in the structure of the judicial institutions. Article 5 of law 4326/2015 abolished paragraph 1 of Article 127B regarding the judicial institution of the first degree of professional football, which started functioning with one member judge, in a way similar to other sports as foreseen in Article 119, while the first-degree judicial institution of the federation remained as a committee composed of three judges according to Article 127B, paragraph 2.

409. Apart from the above, law 4410/2016 added in Article 26 of law 2725/1999, paragraph 7, which as amended with law 5025/2023, provides for the obligation of sports federations to adopt the Code of Deontology (Ethics) following the standards of the respective international federations and the IOC and EFIPID and to establish Ethics Committees composed of three to five members appointed by their Board of Administration. In the First – Degree Institutions should also be included the Primary Disciplinary Committee of EOKAN, competent for doping offences except those under the competency of CAS.

410. Within the frame of the HFF (EPO), other committees also function, which may be considered of judicial nature, such as the Football Player Status Committee that monitors compliance with FIFA's and EPO's players status and transfer regulations and determines the status of football players. It is responsible for the classification of athletes as amateurs or professionals, for the control of supporting documents for the issuance of a sports identity card, the adjudication of appeals against decisions to reject applications for registration or transfer, the maintenance

19. Article 29 of the law 3479/2006, which is no longer valid, provided the possibility of the football authorities to function completely independently, according to the statutes and the regulations of the national and the international federation. In case football or any other sport federation exercised this full autonomy right, it could act even without respecting the provisions and obligations of the law 2725/1999, thus resulting to the loss of the financial support of any kind from the State.
20. For almost one year, during the seasons 2016–2017 the HFF was governed by a Committee appointed by FIFA and UEFA in agreement with the Deputy Minister of Sport, with the task to reorganize in all levels the HFF and Greek football generally.

of the relevant registers and the decision-making on any issue of registration or transfer. Judicial may also be considered the nature of the licensing organs of first and second degree.

§7. The Second-Degree Judicial Instruments

411. The Second-Degree Judicial Instrument for all sports apart from football is ASEAD, which functions under the General Secretariat of Sport and consists of judges, according to Article 123 of law 2725/1999.[21] ASEAD was established with law 75/1975 as a collective institution of public administration, competent for the resolution of disputes of disciplinary, technical and administrative character, as well as for issues that have to do with the application of laws and regulations in the sport activities. Any person, legal or natural, damaged by a decision of a first-degree institution of a sport union or federation or by a decision of its relevant Committee or the Board of Administration for a purely sport matter, such as the registration or the transfer of an athlete, could appeal against this decision within two days in case of disciplinary sanction or eight days in any other case from the notification of the decision.

412. Some years ago, ASEAD also had the responsibility to examine disputes of economic character. This competence was finally entrusted to the Committees for the Settlement of Economic Disputes first with law 1958/1991.

413. According to Article 124 in combination with Articles 121 and 26 ASEAD is competent for appeals against: (i) Board decisions of sports unions, professional leagues and federations, (ii) decisions of organs of the above which do not require validation by the Board related to disciplinary sanctions, registration or transfer of athletes, the classification in the competitions and in general the application of laws and regulations, (iii) decisions of disciplinary organs of associations (clubs) imposing sanctions, if the statutes of the respective federation does not provide any validation procedure, (iv) decisions of the Committee of Sports Spirit, Ethics and Deontology (EFIPID) of the HOC, (v) decisions of the first degree jurisdictional organs of Article 119 in certain sports (basketball, volleyball, handball and water polo) if they are issued over protests or impose matches to be played without spectators or sanction for more than two matches athletes and more than two months coaches, Board members, etc., or impose a fine of more than EUR 5,000 or sanctions provided in the law for breach of provisions related to shareholders, Board members and athletes of AAEs, and (vi) decisions of the Ethics Commissions of the federations. It is also competent for appeals against decisions of the Primary Disciplinary Committee of EOKAN. The appeal before A.S.E.A.D. is exercised by the natural or legal person who suffers direct or indirect damage from the First Instance decision.

---

21. *See* above para. 31.

414. The deadline for exercising the appeal is eight days, and in case of appeal against a decision of the First-Degree Disciplinary Organ, it is two days and starts from the day after notification or knowledge of the contested decision in any way. The exercise of the appeal does not suspend the execution of the contested decision.

415. The special local section of ASEAD of Thessaloniki is responsible for adjudicating appeals: (a) against decisions of the Board of Administration of the sports associations based in the administrative regions of Epirus, Thessaly, Central Macedonia, Western Macedonia, Eastern Macedonia and Thrace or against the decisions of their statutory bodies if these do not require ratification by their administrative boards, (b) against the decisions of disciplinary organs of associations (clubs) imposing sanctions if they are seated in the administrative regions of Epirus, Thessaly, Macedonia and Thrace, (c) against the decisions of the first-instance local judicial bodies of seated in Thessaloniki.

416. The Second-Degree Judicial Instrument for football is, according to Article 127B, paragraph 3, the Appeal Committee of EPO (HFF), composed of judges as well, with the same competencies as ASEAD, except for the appeals against the decisions of EFIPID, which are always judged by ASEAD. It functions according to the provisions of EPO Statutes and the respective regulations and is competent for appeals against decisions of the first-degree disciplinary organs in case they impose relegation, deduction of more than one point from classification, stadium closure for more than a match, fine above a certain amount depending on the division of the club, sanction of more than a match for players, coaches, etc., or they decide on protests as well as against decisions of the Ethics Commission. The deadline for exercising the appeal is two working days for decisions of the First-Degree Organs of the Professional Leagues and EPO and five days from the notification of decisions of the competent bodies of the unions. It is composed of five members and meets in the presence of three, among whom is the President or Deputy President. EPO Statutes and regulations provide that decisions of the EPO Appeal Committee may be appealed in the Court of Arbitration for Sport (CAS)

§8. Other Judicial Institutions of Arbitrary Nature

I. Committees for the Settlement of Economic Disputes

417. Disputes of economic nature between athletes or coaches and associations or federations may be settled as follows: disputes between amateur athletes and associations or federations or between coaches and federations are obligatorily settled by the tribunal of the seat of the association or the federation. Disputes between coaches and amateur associations may be settled by a Committee that functions within the gulfs of the federation if foreseen in the coaches' regulation of the respective sport.

418. Regarding professional sports (football, basketball and volleyball), there is a provision in Article 95 of law 2725/1999 for the foundation and the function of first and second-degree Committees for the Settlement of Economic Disputes, the exact competence of which will be the settlement of all disputes of economic character between professional athletes or coaches and their TAA or AAEs, that may arise from their contracts.

419. The similar provisions of the previous law 1958/1991 caused discussions about their constitutionality and regarding the issue of whether these committees could have been considered as obligatory arbitration institutions. In order to solve this, after the modification of Article 95 of law 2725/1999 with laws 3057/2002, 3262/2004 and 4049/2012, the law defines that 'in case there is no explicit condition in the work contract between the athlete, the coach and the team, these committees function as institutions of arbitrational resolution of disputes and their decisions can be executed according to Article 904 paragraph 2 of the Greek Civil Procedure (arbitrational decisions).'

420. The first-degree Committees for the Settlement of Economic Disputes function within the gulfs of the relevant professional league, while the second-degree ones are in the relevant sport federation. They all consist of five members, among whom are three judges, one representative of the relevant professional league or federation and one representative of the athletes', respectively coaches', association.

421. Especially in football, regardless of the law provision, both the first and second-degree committees function within EPO. The First-Degree Committee for the Settlement of Economic Disputes is composed of two active judges (President and Deputy President), two members representing the athletes appointed by the Panhellenic Association of Paid Football Players, two members representing the clubs appointed by the professional leagues and two members representing coaches appointed by the coaches' association.

A. Football Arbitration Court

422. EPO Statutes and regulations also provide the establishment of the Football Arbitration Court. It is the second-degree institution for the settlement of economic disputes, competent for the appeals against the First-Degree Committee, but it is also competent for appeals against decisions of the Players Status Committee and for the settlement of any dispute between AAEs, professional leagues, unions, associations and players or intermediaries which do not fall under the competence of other committees, disputes related to competitions and to elections in unions or leagues, etc.

423. It is composed of judges and arbitrators appointed in lists by football stakeholders (leagues, unions, players, coaches) and meets with five or three members depending on the case.

B. *Court of Arbitration for Sport*

424. The CAS is an international body established in 1984 to settle disputes related to sport through arbitration. It is also competent for appeals against decisions of international and national federations, national Olympic committees and other international or national institutions. Its headquarters are in Lausanne. Recently, it has been included in sports justice institutions for EPO and EOE because they both have provisions in their statutes that disputes are finally settled in CAS.

C. *The Sport Public Prosecutor*

425. Article 128, which was added to law 2725/1999 with Article 50 of law 3057/2002, sets out that the Head of the Attorney's District Office of Athens, Piraeus and Thessaloniki nominates a Sport Public Prosecutor, whose competence is to prosecute those who commit sport crimes, to supervise the police works for the confrontation of violence in the sport fields and to be responsible for the right application of the relevant penal legal provisions. A prosecutor of the Supreme Court who is especially nominated by the Head Supreme Court Prosecutor coordinates the work of the Sport Public Prosecutors.

II. Philatelic Sports Spirit, Ethics and Deontology Committee

426. The EFIPID, former Committee of Sport Spirit EFIP, former Committee of Sport Quality, was founded in the middle of the twentieth century, playing at that period an important role in the conservation of the sport spirit and the principles of sport which we inherited from the antiquity. It had the right to sanction all athletes, coaches, referees, administrators, and even spectators by depriving them of the right to participate in any way in the sports activity in case they committed serious offences against the spirit of sport. Its authority decreased when professionalism was established in some sports, since they created their own disciplinary mechanisms.

427. This Committee, whose necessity today is questionable, functions as an institution of the HOC, according to Article 130 of law 2725/1999.

428. The purpose and the competence of EFIPHD is the infliction of disciplinary sanctions on those who violate the principles of the sport spirit, the traditions and the Olympic Ideal, as they are set out in the IOC Chart and in the Regulation of Sport Quality, established with a royal decree of 1955.

429. EFIPID takes action either ex officio or after a denunciation. Particularly in football, it takes action only after the remand of the relevant judicial institutions. The appeals against the decisions of EFIPID are discussed in ASEAD, according to Article 124, paragraph D of law 2725/1999.

430. According to Article 12 of the Statutes of the HOC, it: (a) imposes sanctions on anyone guilty of violating the spirit of sportsmanship and the fundamental principles and rules of sports ethics and conduct, in accordance with the current legislation, the Olympic Charter, the regulations of the IOC, and its regulations approved by the Plenary Session; (b) exercises any other authority related to the spirit of sports fandom, the principles and rules of sports ethics and ethics assigned to it by the law or the Plenary Assembly of the E.O.E. by its decision.

431. EFIPID is taken after a formal complaint or after a decision of the Plenary session or ex officio in the following cases in particular: (a) use of prohibited substances and methods of drug stimulation (doping), confirmed by a finding – decision of the competent state authority; (b) irrevocable citation, by summons or will and conviction, to any penalty, for the supply or marketing of prohibited substances and methods or other violation of existing doping laws, violation of drug laws, crime against sexual freedom, sports offence violence, manipulation or altering the result of a match, bribery – bribery of sports actors, forgery with the aim of misleading the sports authorities; (c) violation of the Code of the IOC to prevent match manipulation; (d) violation of the right to freely participate in sporting activity; (e) verbal or practical display of disrespect for diversity (race, colour, language, sex, religious, political or other beliefs, etc.); (f) violation of the provisions of the statute of the E.O.E. and its internal regulations, with the aim of obtaining a personal benefit or preventing participation in the governing bodies of a sports organization or preventing participation in competitions; (g) any other violation of sports fan spirit, competitive and sports ethics.

432. It is obvious that the disciplinary competence of EFIPHD goes beyond the disciplinary competence of the sport federations and can be considered more as a collective administrative instrument that imposes administrative sanctions rather than a disciplinary judicial institution itself.

Part II. Sport and Employment[22]

Chapter 1. General Issues

433. Sport is a contest of special technical corporal activity, the goal of which is the highest corporal capacity and, finally, the victory. The specificity and the technical nature of sport, the way the organization of the events, the participation in those and the relations among the athletes, the coaches, the referees and the sport institutions are defined by the rules of the sport and the legal provisions of the national and international sports law.

434. Regardless of the specificity of sport, it is undeniable that general rules of labour law apply in part of sports activity, especially in professional sports. Greek labour law recognizes three kinds of contracts which could be considered applicable in professional sports activity.

§1. The Dependent Labour Contract

435. A contract of dependent labour is an agreement between an employer and an employee, based on which the employee undertakes the main obligation to provide his work to the employer under his supervision and control, and the employer the main obligation to pay the salary. The criterion that characterizes a contract as a contract of dependent labour is personal dependence, which manifests itself in the right of the employer to give instructions to the employee regarding the manner, place and time of providing his services and to exercise supervision and control to ascertain of the employee's compliance with his instructions, regardless of whether the employer actually exercises this right or leaves room for initiative to the employee.

§2. The Project Contract

436. A project contract exists when a person (contractor) undertakes against another person (employer/owner of the project) the obligation to perform a certain

22. Elements in this part are taken from the work of D. Panagiotopoulos, *Sport Law, Systematic View – Application*, 2005, 355 et seq., K. Christodoulou, *Sports Law*, 2023, 63 et seq., D. Goulas, *Employment Relationship of Athletes*, 2014, 19 et seq.

project for a fee. The main element that distinguishes the work contract from the project contract is that in the case of the work contract, the provision of the work is of interest regardless of a specific result, while in the case of the project contract, the result of the execution of a certain project is of interest.

§3. The Independent Services Contract

437. A contract for the provision of independent services exists when the provider of independent services undertakes the obligation towards a person to provide work without being subject to the supervision and control of his counterparty. The main characteristic, therefore, of the contract for the provision of independent services is the development of initiative and independence in determining the place, time and manner of providing the work, which is basically not the case in the case of the contract of dependent work.

438. It is a common trend of both legal theory and jurisprudence to consider the majority of the agreements related to employment as Dependent Labour Contracts.

Chapter 2. Sources of Employment Law

439. The main source of Employment (Labour) Law in Greece is the law including:

(a) The EU Treaty and the respective EU directives and regulations.
(b) The Constitution, which contains respective provisions in Articles 22 and 23. Article 22, paragraph 1 provides that: 'Work is a right and is protected by the State, which ensures the creation of employment condition for all citizens and the moral and material elevation of the working rural and urban population. All employees regardless of gender or other discrimination, have the right to equal pay for work of equal value.'
(c) The law, including the respective articles of the CC and the special law for employment.
(d) The Collective Bargain Agreements, as well as the arbitrary decisions and work regulations.

§1. Legal Status of Players – Amateur Athletes

440. Two are the basic elements that define the legal status of athletes: The registration to a federation as an athlete and the legal status of the association, TAA or AAE to which he/she belongs.

441. An athlete is de facto whoever systematically cultivates sports and reaches noteworthy results. Simple body exercise though is not enough by itself to define someone as a de facto athlete.

442. According to Greek sport law, athletes are considered those who obtain a legal licence by the sport federation of the sport they practise, proving in most sports that they belong to a sport association. By issuing this licence, every athlete can participate alone or with the team of his association in all official competitions organized by the relevant sport federation.

443. Athletes are divided into three categories: (a) the amateurs, (b) the paid athletes, who are connected to a sport association that avails a TAA with a contract of work, and (c) the professional athletes, who are connected to an AAE with a contract of work.

444. Article 33 of law 2725/1999 as amended provides the status of amateur athletes. In paragraph 1, it is clearly mentioned that 'the provisions of this article apply to athletes who do not compete in the paid athletes section of a sports association or in an AAE and to veteran athletes, i.e., those who have reached the age limit stated in the regulations of the relevant federation, who are required to have a sports card and athlete's health card and are subject to the regulations of article 27 of the relevant sports federation'.

445. In the field of amateur sport, each athlete is in principle free to choose his sport association, which he can join as an athlete, and consequently, he can acquire the sports card through this association in order to exercise himself physically and to participate in the sport events.

446. For the registration of the athlete to the records of the sport federation and the acquisition of the sports card, some requirements are foreseen in the law as well as in the regulations of the federations. Among those very important is the athlete's health card, a copy of his/her ID card and of course pictures that are to be stuck on the sports card in order to enable the referees to check in every event the athletes' identity.

447. By obtaining the sports card, the amateur athlete avails of the sport quality in a real sense since he does not offer his sport services with the aim of earning money. The issuing of the sports card is proof of the agreement between the athlete and the sport association that this athlete is obliged to offer his sport services to the association without any salary. This agreement may not be included in any of the main kinds of contracts mentioned above, but has the meaning that the athlete is obliged – although usually there are no consequences in case he freely decides to stop it – to take part in the training of the team and the sport events without being entitled to any kind of salary. His only reward is the improvement of his capabilities, his personal development, and his moral satisfaction. Beyond this, with this agreement, every athlete assumes the dangers of each sport on condition that the respective technical regulations are followed.

448. On the contrary, the sport association has the responsibility to secure the required technical infrastructure for the needs of training. It also assumes the financial means required for the training and the expenses required for the participation of its athletes in the games (e.g., transport expenses, etc.). It even undertakes the expenses for possible injuries of the athlete during the training or a match.

449. Paragraph 2 of Article 33 provides that 'Without prejudice to the provisions of article 85 of this law (referred to athletes offering their services to TAA or sports limited companies), the competitive activity of athletes does not constitute the exercise of professional sports activity.' Financial or other benefits given by sports clubs, associations or federations to athletes to support their sports activity do not constitute financial consideration within the meaning of the provisions of Article 86 of this law. They are just the means for the athletes to be able to come up against the size of the physical exercise, the training and the matches.

450. Nevertheless, the distinction between an amateur and a professional athlete is not very easy. The criteria chosen by law regarding the distinction between amateur and professional athletes is not correct. Not only because only men's top divisions in football, basketball and volleyball include the participation of TAA or AAEs, meaning that in all other sports as well as in all-female sports, all athletes are in principle amateur, but also because they ignore the reality that differentiates amateur from professional athletes. Systematic occupation, devotion to the effort, focus on the result, frequency of the training and matches, percentage of the time on a daily basis spent and of course income should be seriously taken into consideration.

451. Nowadays, it is commonplace for amateur athletes to receive financial benefits from their associations. These benefits are much more than a simple financial support for the coverage of the athletes' basic needs. They are usually paid like a salary at the end of the month. What is more, in many cases, a promissory note may also be signed by the association to the order of the athlete, usually as a guarantee for the deposit of the agreed amount, which the athlete has to return after the payment of the amount owed to him. In these cases, the Greek courts have judged that there is a de facto hidden work relation between the association and the athlete, regardless of the fact that the athlete is supposed to be an amateur, nonpaid one.

452. Recent amendment in the sports law with 4603/2019 included in Article 33, paragraph 2 a new provision that 'Male and female athletes who compete in associations that participate in amateur championships of national categories of team sports, men and women, may sign a private agreement for the provision of sports services, which is submitted to the relevant sports federation.' This does not clarify the whole situation because it only refers to team sports and does not classify those athletes as professionals, but it definitely restricts the inaccuracy of the law, which must be further amended to reflect the reality. Such agreements should rather be considered as independent services contracts and not dependent labour contracts.[23]

453. Apart from the above, Article 33, paragraph 4 provides that an individual or team sports athlete is allowed to enter into sponsorship or advertising contracts for products or services with a natural or legal person as long as this does not contradict the technical regulations of the sport, the regulations of the relevant sports federation or the IOC. The contracts of the previous paragraph are required to be approved by the relevant sports federation and to be submitted to the competent tax authorities. If one of the conditions is not met, the contracts are void and do not produce legal effects.

454. The relations between amateur athletes and sports associations, as well as the terms and the conditions of the registration and the transfers of athletes, the period for their operation and the competent institutions for them, are set out for every sport by the statutes and the special regulations of the federation, according to Article 27 in combination with Article 33 of law 2725/1999.

455. According to paragraph 3 of Article 33, transfers are allowed to take place in one or two transfer periods each year, with the exception of transfers of Greek athletes abroad, for which another transfer period can be defined. The duration of each transfer period cannot exceed sixty days. An athlete of an association who is

23. K. Christodoulou, *Sports Law*, 2023, 76–77.

transferred to a team abroad without his association's consent belongs de jure to the same association once he returns to Greece, according to paragraph 10 of the same article.

456. The regulations of the federations include provisions for the conditions of transfer due to release, competitive inactivity, relocation of the athlete for studies or for professional reasons of him or his parents, due to free transfer of an athlete under or over a certain age and due to dissolution of an association or suspension of its department's activity or loss of its special athletic recognition. The agreement to transfer an athlete from one sports association to another, with the consent of the former, is also allowed with financial consideration as long as the appropriate tax document is issued for the granting of the athlete's sports card with the corresponding value added tax or any other tax charge that provided for by the current legislation and registered in the Books of Income and Expenditure of the two sports associations.

457. In the transfer regulations of the federations, it is usually foreseen that athletes are free to transfer without the consent of their previous association in cases such as the following: (a) in case the athlete is released from his previous association; (b) in case he/she has not participated in any event for a period no less than two years; (c) in case the athlete has moved from his/her hometown to another place more than 200 km away, for educational or professional reasons, personal or from his/her parents; (d) in case of disassembly of the association or of suspension of its function or due to the loss of its special sports recognition. It has been judged that the loss of the association's right to vote is equal to the loss of its special sport recognition and gives the athlete the right to be freely transferred.

458. In the same, regulations may be set as necessary conditions for the approval of the transfer of athletes to amateur associations without the consent of their previous ones, such as: (a) the athlete, during the last two competitive periods, not to have participated in a national team, and (b) not to have been punished according to the provisions of the sport law for denial to offer his sport services to the national teams.

459. A quite realistic and, in accordance with the constitutional provisions mentioned above,[24] a recent amendment introduced paragraph 3A in Article 33, following which: (i) any upper age limit provided by a sports federation regulation for the issuance of an athlete's card is void and (ii) the amateur athlete is freely transferred from the sports association to which he belongs, to another club, from the summer transfer period of the calendar year in which he turns 19 years of age and after.

460. This solved an issue frequently dealt with in the past by ASEAD. According to its decisions, important reasons justifying the transfer of the athlete without consent of their previous associations can be considered additionally, even if not foreseen in the regulations, the following: (a) family and professional reasons, (b)

24. *See* paras 229 et seq.

studies, (c) change of residence, (d) other conditions characterizing the sport activity, such as the disruption of the relations between the athlete and his coach, the isolation of the athlete.

461. The above decisions initiated a discussion on whether the right of the natural person to choose freely to which association he would like to join prevails from the rights of the associations to expect to be rewarded from transfer fees for their investments. This led some federations to provide in their regulations the obligation to the association that registers an athlete without consent of his/her previous club to pay a certain amount following an algorithm to the federation, which then would compensate the old association of the athlete with it or most of it. Especially in football, a complex system of solidarity and training compensation to the clubs that have trained the players until a certain age is included in the FIFA Regulations on the Status and Transfer of Players, which recently has also been applied at the national level as inserted in the respective regulations of EPO. The recent law amendment terminates the discussion in favour of the freedom of the adult athletes to choose to which club they register or transfer but leaves it open for the regulations to define a compensation to the athlete's old club.

462. The instrument competent to judge on the acceptance or the rejection of the transfer of an athlete is a special committee formed by the relevant sport federation. The Board of Administration of the federation ratifies the decision of the special committee. Such decisions of the federations can be appealed to ASEAD, according to Articles 121 and 123–127 of law 2725/1999, while for football, the Football Arbitration Court.

463. Another issue for both amateur and professional players which makes their status more complicated is the obligation to participate in the national teams. Article 33, paragraph 5 includes a provision that the offer of services to the national teams is the highest obligation of the athletes. An athlete who unreasonably refuses to offer his services to the respective national team is punished, in accordance with what is defined in the special regulation of the federation, with the penalty of exclusion from the matches of the national team, the championships and the cup and is deprived of all kinds of benefits of the federation. An athlete who is punished for refusing to offer his services to the national team is also deprived of all kinds of State benefits, the benefits provided by the provisions of this article and any special tax exemptions. It is not clear whether this issue of purely sports nature,[25] which causes mandatory deprivation of the athlete's services to his/her club through law enforcement and regulation within the monopolistic and pyramidal structure of sport[26] and without the consent of the association which is given a priori with the registration in the federation or in a competition should be considered as establishing a three parties Special Contract or a separate Dependent Labour Contract between the athlete and the federation or Independent Services Contract or even an agreement similar to the one between an amateur athlete and his/her association. It

25. *See* decision Deliege of the European Court, C-51/96 and C-191/97.
26. D. Goulas, *Employment Relationships of Athletes*, 2014, 459.

seems that the last option is the closest to reality, considering the fact that in most cases, no contract is signed between the federation and the athlete.

464. Another issue dealt with by the law in paragraph 7 of Article 33 is the limitations on the right of athletes to be registered in an association depending on their nationality. The law as amended provides that in the Greek amateur championships at local, regional or national level and in the Greek amateur cup competitions, in both individual and team sports, the following are allowed to participate: (a) expatriates (Greeks leaving abroad), (b) citizens of a Member State of the EU, (c) citizens of a third country and stateless persons, who legally reside in the country with a valid residence permit or residence card, and (d) citizens of a third country or stateless persons residing in the country either as beneficiaries of international protection or as applicants for international protection. The above persons are registered in sports clubs of their choice and acquire sports status as long as they meet the age and other conditions set by the regulations of the relevant federation and are not registered at the same time in a sports club of another EU Member State or a third country.

§2. Paid and Professional Athletes: Employment Relationship – Fundamental Rights and Obligations for Clubs and Players

465. As mentioned in the above paragraphs, the sport law makes a clear distinction between the amateur and the professional sport quality (Article 90, paragraph 1), defining that the sport activity of athletes cannot be considered as professional activity (Article 33, paragraph 2) unless the athlete has signed a contract with a TAA or an AAE resulting on him/her becoming a paid or a professional athlete (Article 85, paragraphs 1 and 2).

466. Amateur athletes' sport quality is in principle incompatible with the acquirement of financial benefits or the amelioration of their financial condition. On the contrary, the paid and professional athletes maintain the sport quality, although they take part in the sport activity with the aim of earning money. These athletes possess the sport quality to have the right to participate in the games. Therefore, these athletes avail of the sport quality in plasma of law.

467. The categories of athletes paid for offering their sport services consist of the paid and the professional athletes. A paid athlete is whoever signs a work contract with an association availing of a TAA, that is to say, only in men's basketball and volleyball. A professional athlete is anyone who signs a work contract with an AAE, that is to say only in men's football and basketball. Article 85, paragraph 3 provides a third category of paid or professional athletes, those who are under contract for at least one more year with a TAA or AAE that relegates to an amateur division, who according to Article 94, keep their status for one more season, although they belong to an amateur association.

468. Special provisions define the terms and the details for the paid and the professional athletes, according to Articles 85 et seq. of law 2725/1999. A special regulation is issued according to Article 87 for every professional sport (football, basketball, volleyball), based on the agreement of the relevant sport federation, the relevant professional league and the athletes' association, defining the relations between the paid or the professional athletes and the TAA or the AAEs where they belong and in particular the conditions for the acquirement of the quality of the paid or professional athlete.

469. Generally, it is regulated that for the acquirement of the sports card for the paid and professional athletes, a contract must be signed between the athlete and the TAA or the AAE and submitted to the relevant professional league or federation for approval. Further requirements, such as pictures or health card, are foreseen in the abovementioned regulations, while for athletes that do not possess Greek nationality or belong to a club from another country, an international transfer certificate approved by the relevant international federation according to its regulations is necessary.

470. Another special regulation defines the categories of these athletes, the number of these athletes for each TAA or AAE, the conditions for the registration, the transfer and the release of these athletes, the time, the procedure and the competent instruments, as well as any relevant issue, according to Article 88, paragraph 1 of law 2725/1999.

471. Law clearly provides in Article 85 that the contract of the paid or professional athletes is a Dependent Labour Contract for offering sports services. So, the offering of sport services is according to the sport law an offering of dependent work and the relevant contract is ruled by the provisions of the labour law and the sports law.

472. It is worth mentioning that after the *Bosman* case, the provisions of the European law concerning professional athletes are also applied to amateur athletes when a contract of dependent work of a financial nature is hidden. Such decisions that have recognized the relationship between amateur sport athletes and their associations as a working contract have been issued by the Greek civil courts. These decisions are usually justified on the basis that the high-level athletes in sports not recognized by the law as professional (the law recognizes as professional sports only football, basketball and volleyball's man-high divisions) spend many hours every day in training, and they receive quite big amounts of money for their sport activity or from sponsoring contracts; therefore they should be considered professionals.

473. In the contract between a paid athlete and a TAA and between a professional athlete and an AAE, the provisions of the labour law apply (Article 85, paragraph 4), but with the necessary adaptions due to the specificity of sports, such as the obligation to offer their services in various times and days not known when signing the contract.

474. The duration of a paid or professional athlete contract may not be smaller than six months and bigger than five years. Minor athletes aged less than 18 may sign contracts for only up to three years.

475. Athletes connected to an association or to a limited company with a contract to offer sport services receive regular fees, freely agreed with the contract and within the framework of the relevant regulations. It is regulated though that the salary in any case should not be lower than the monthly salary of an unskilled worker set out in the National Collective Bargaining Agreement. In practice, especially in football, the players receive the minimum salary because this is payable fourteen times per year (twelve months plus bonuses for Christmas, Easter and holidays). The remaining amount is agreed to be a fixed fee payable in instalments.

476. Athletes may also receive extra bonuses, which are included in the contract or set out freely by a decision of the TAA or the AAE before the beginning of the championships.

477. The main obligations of the clubs arising from the athletes' contracts are:

- The Club is obliged to pay out to the Player's monthly salary, at the latest at the end of each month, twelve months per year.
- Apart from the aforementioned monthly salary, the Club is obliged to pay the Player Christmas bonus (one monthly salary) and Easter Bonus (half of the monthly salary), as well as the Holiday Benefit (half of the monthly salary).
- The Club is obliged to protect the Player's human rights and deter discrimination against the Player.
- The Club is obliged to maintain a record of the injuries and illnesses of the Player, always in respect of privacy and personal information. The record is maintained and kept by the competent team medical doctor.
- The Club is obliged to cover the pension contributions and social security expenses, as foreseen by the law, promptly and fully paid.
- The Club is obliged to provide medical insurance as foreseen by the Regulations by a personal or group insurance policy contract.
- The Club may exploit exclusively the rights from the image of the Player to the extent that they serve as part of its whole image.

478. The main obligations of the athlete are:

- To participate in the matches to the best of his abilities when selected to play.
- To participate in the training sessions and the preparations for a match, pursuant to the instructions of the technical staff.
- To join the national teams of his country whenever asked by the national federation.
- To lead a healthy way of life, maintaining his physical condition at high levels.
- To comply with and act pursuant to the instructions of those being responsible for the team. (e.g., to the extent that is reasonable, e.g., stay at a place that serves the purposes of the Club.).

- To participate in the Club activities, including sporting, social and commercial ones.
- To obey the regulations of the Club (including the by-laws that have been notified to him duly prior to the execution of the contract, if applicable.).
- To behave in the spirit of sportsmanship to people involved in matches and training, know the rules of the game and accept the decisions of match officials.
- To abstain from and not participate in other sports activities, activities of other types or general dangerous activities that have not been previously approved by the Club and are not covered by the Club insurance.
- To take care of the Club property and return it past the end of the contract.
- To notify the Club immediately in the event of illness or accident and not undergo any type of medical therapy without prior knowledge of the team doctor.
- To undergo regular medical tests and care, following the request of the doctor.
- To avoid involvement in doping or betting activity.
- Not to bring the Club or the sport in general to disrepute.

In case of violation of the above obligations, on behalf of the club, the athlete may address the competent committee, claim any owed amount, or even proceed to termination of his contract for just cause. In case of a breach on behalf of the player, the club may impose sanctions as foreseen in the law and in the internal regulations, such as a reprimand, a fine, or the termination of the contracts for just cause. The competent judiciary institutions for the disputes that arise from the contracts between professional or paid athletes and the AAEs and the TAA regarding their validity, their termination, the athletes' financial claims, the violation of their obligations, etc., are the Committees for the Resolution of Financial Disputes.

§3. Legal Status of Coaches, Referees, Managers

I. Coaches

479. The exercise of the profession of a coach is regulated in Article 31, which is amended several times and the newly introduced Article 31A and 31B of law 2725/1999.

480. According to Article 31, paragraph 1, a coach of a sport is a professional who undertakes, at a competitive level and for competitive purposes, the preparation, guidance, increase in sports performance, sports progress and the development of the abilities of athletes.

481. In the past, the General Secretariat of Sports used to issue professional coach licences to those who fulfilled the criteria set by the law. Following an amendment with law 4908/2022 today, exercising the profession of coach is only permitted to the professional who, following announcement to the General Secretariat of Sports (G.G.A.) and on condition that he/she meets the conditions for practising the profession, receives an individual registration number and is registered in the electronic register of coaches, held at the G.G.A. Registration in the electronic register of coaches is notified to the relevant sports federation and the relevant coaches' association.

482. According to paragraph 4, sports federations and sports associations, AAEs and TAA in every sport, individual or team, Olympic or non-Olympic, are obliged to employ a coach for every sport they cultivate and for all sections, of all ages and competition categories.[27] The obligation to employ a coach does not apply: (a) to sports associations that cultivate the sports of chess, competitive bridge, motor sports and aerobatic sports, (b) during the first two years from the affiliation of a sport to a recognized sports federation, for sports associations that cultivate this sport, and (c) during the first two years from the granting of special sports recognition to a sports federation for its member sports associations.

483. Every coach must agree in writing with the sports body to which he provides his services and sign a contract of full-time, part-time or periodic employment, dependent labour or provision of independent services. His salary cannot be lower than EUR 250 per month of service provided, regardless of the type of contract signed. Every sports body is obliged to employ a coach for a period of at least six months within the twelve-month period from 1 August to 31 July of the following year. Anyone who holds a licence to practise the profession of coach from the G.G.A. cannot maintain his athlete status and compete in official competitions of the sport for which he holds a professional licence unless he has filed his licence with the relevant sports federation. An active athlete of a team sport or an individual sport who holds a licence to practise the profession of coaching may exceptionally practise the profession of coaching in: (a) another competition category than the one in which he participates as an athlete, (b) academies, or (c) teams of the opposite sex of any competitive category. Exceptions are provided for the coach of equestrian and shooting.

484. Article 31A provides the classification of coaches into three categories as follows:

(1) The coaches are divided into A', B' and C' level from the highest to the lowest, according to their education and qualifications, as follows:
   (a) Level A sports coaches. This level includes: (i) the higher education graduates of the Schools or Departments of Science of Physical Education and Sports (S.E.F.A.A. or T.E.F.A.A.) or the holders of a higher education degree from a foreign school that has been recognized as equal and equivalent specialized in the respective sport, (ii) the higher education

27. The validity of para. 4 of Art. 31, regarding the obligation to employ a coach begins on 1 Jul. 2024. Until then, coaches are obliged to employ: (a) the sports federations and sports unions, (b) the AAEs and the TAA, (c) the sports associations that cultivate team sports and participate in national championships and in a local first-class championship, and (d) the sports associations that cultivate individual sports and have athletes under the age of 18.

graduates of S.E.F.A.A. or T.E.F.A.A., or the holders of a higher education degree from a foreign school that has been recognized as equal and equivalent regardless of speciality and with a professional experience of at least three years as B-level coaches of the specific sport, (iii) the holders of a diploma from the periodic coaching school of the General Secretariat of Sports (G.G.A.) A' level of the sport or a corresponding level of diploma of the National Coaching School of G.G.A, and (iv) former athletes who have participated in summer or winter Olympic Games or have won 1st to 6th victory in a World Championship or 1st to 4th victory in a European Championship for men or women, as well as the coaches of athletes who won the above distinctions in these events, with proof of successful attendance at an A-level coaching school.

(b) Level B sports coaches. This level includes: (i) the higher education graduates of S.E.F.A.A. or T.E.F.A.A., or the holders of a higher education degree from a foreign school, which has been recognized as equal and equivalent regardless of speciality, as long as they have been successfully taught the sport as a subject based on the study certificate, (ii) the higher education graduates of S.E.F.A.A. or T.E.F.A.A. or the holders of a higher education degree from a foreign school, which has been recognized as equal and equivalent regardless of speciality and with at least three years of professional experience as coaches at level C of the specific sport, (iii) the higher education graduates of S.E.F.A.A. or T.E.F.A.A. or the holders of a higher education degree from a foreign school, which has been recognized as equal and equivalent regardless of speciality, as long as he has completed at least seven competitive seasons in the top division of the respective sport as an athlete. The confirmation of the sporting activity is given by the respective federation, (iv) the holders of a Level B Coaching School diploma of the specific sport of the periodic coaching schools of the G.G.A. or equivalent diploma level of the National School of Coaches of the G.G.A.

(c) Level C sports coaches. This level includes: (i) the holders of the C' level Coaching School diploma of the specific sport of the periodic coaching schools of the G.G.A. or equivalent diploma level of the National School of Coaches of the G.G.A., (ii) holders of a certified diploma from a Scientific Training Institute (IEK), or a corresponding recognized foreign school.

485. Holders of a coaching licence are employed according to their level as follows:

(a) Holders of an A' level coaching licence 'in any AAE, TAA, amateur sports association or academy, as well as in the National Team as federal coaches in all categories.
(b) B level coach licence holders are employed in any amateur club or academy, as well as assistant coaches to A level coaches.

(c) Holders of a C' level coaching licence are employed: (i) as assistant coaches in cases where B level coaches can be employed as first coaches, as well as (ii) as first coaches in academies.[28]

486. Especially for the sport of football, the professional rights of coaches according to their level are determined by the Hellenic Football Association (E.P.O.), according to the UEFA-E.P.O. Coaching Agreement, as well as according to the Football Coaches Regulation.

487. At the General Secretariat of Sport (G.G.A.), a school named 'National Coaching School' (E.S.P.) is established, responsible for the training of coaches of all levels for all sports. The E.S.P. has the following responsibilities: (a) recommends the establishment of individual coaching schools per sport or sport discipline to the competent body of the G.G.A. (b) coordinates the educational work and operation of individual coaching schools per sport or sport branch, (c) prepares and recommends the training program for coaches, (d) recommends to the Minister of Sport the issuance and content of the notice of participation in the individual coaching schools, (e) selects the teaching staff who train and examine the coaches. Trainers certified by the national anti-doping body are selected for anti-doping training.

488. The E.S.P. consists of seven regular members, with an equal number of substitutes, who are appointed for a four-year term by the decision of the Minister of Sport. The president and his deputy are senior officials of the G.G.A., three regular members and their deputies are employees of the G.G.A., and three regular members with their deputies are members of the Teaching Research Staff (DEP) of the Schools or Departments of Science of Physical Education and Sports (S.E.F.A.A. or T.E.F.A.A.), proposed by S.E.F.A.A. or T.E.F.A.A. Football, water skiing and skiing coaching schools may be established and operated by the relevant sports federations.

II. Referees

489. Referees are the individuals who are responsible for the surveillance of the holding of each event from the sporting point of view according to the rules of the game of the relevant sport and the regulations of the international and national federations. Several names are used for the referees and their assistants in different sports, such as judge referee, line judge, and secretary, as well as for the representative of the organizer, such as delegate, supervisor, commissar, observer, etc.

490. Law 2725/1999 regulates in principle the function of all kinds of referees from administrative and disciplinary points of view.

---

28. The validity of para. 2 of Art. 31A, regarding the employment of a coach depending on the level of the professional licence, begins on 1 Jul. 2024.

491. Referees in team sports are organized in regional associations, according to the provisions of the CC, called referees' associations. For each sport, only one referees' association is permitted (Article 43 of law 2725/1999) within the region of competence of each sport union (Article 11). Only referees with an official diploma and permanent inhabitants of the region of competence of the association can become members of it. The Deputy Minister of Sport or even some other instrument authorized by him gives the referees' association the special recognition, which is required according to Article 43, paragraph 2. In this case, a positive opinion of the relevant federation, as well as a certification from the relevant sport union, is required.

492. The referees' associations prepare the lists of the referees in action or of the retired ones for the local championships and submit them to the highest referee authority of each federation, organize the exams for the referees of the local championships and their education, always under the supervision of the relevant referees' federation (Article 43A, paragraph 3 of law 2725/1999).

493. Only one referees' federation is allowed to be established for each team sport after a decision of the General Assembly of at least five recognized referees' associations, according to Article 43A, paragraph 1 of law 2725/1999. This federation is the supreme institution, and it also functions in the legal form of an association, according to the provisions of the CC. It enjoys, similar to the referees' associations, an administrative, financial and managerial autonomy.

494. The referees' federations are recognized by a special decision of the Minister of Sport or of another authorized instrument of the central or regional administration upon agreement of the relevant sport federation. Their competencies are: (a) the organization of schools for referees and the appointment of teachers to these schools, (b) the submission of lists of referees in action for the games of the national divisions and of retired referees to the relevant sport federation, (c) the nomination of teachers of referees, and (d) the organization of the exams for the referees of the national divisions.

495. According to Article 43A, in championships where AAEs participate, representatives of the referees' associations entitled to elect the members of the Board of Administration of the relevant referees' federation can only be retired referees. If a referee in action votes in the above elections, he/she is excluded from the lists of referees of all the divisions of championships until the term of the Board of Administration comes to an end. Law 5025/2023 introduced an exception to this provision for football.

496. Every sport federation that cultivates a team sport settles down a refereeing regulation, according to Article 44. This regulation has to guarantee the principles of the clarity of the procedures and of the equality among the competitors and to secure that the referees' task will remain uninfluenced.

497. A central refereeing commission functions in the gulfs of every sport federation, both in team and individual sports, according to Article 45, paragraph 2. Its task is the approval of the lists, the evaluation of the referees, the appointment of referees for all competitions, the disciplinary control of the referees, as well as the regulation of all referee-related matters from the sporting point of view.

498. The provisions of the sport law that set out impediments are valid for the referees, as well as the observers, the supervisors, the chronometers and for every other person exercising a work of arbitration or judgment.

The referees' associations and the central refereeing commissions also apply to the individual sports, according to Article 45 of law 2725/1999.

The referees may not be considered under labour or work contracts or independent services contracts with the federations. They are paid by the federations or the associations, but the amount they receive is not considered a fee but as compensation. The only exception to that would be the professional referees provided in Article 48 for sports with the participation of AAEs, that is to say, for football and basketball. This provision has not yet been put into effect. When it comes though in effect the professional referees will sign independent services contract with the federation or the professional league, and they will receive the agreed amount as a fee.

III. Managers

499. Individuals who act administratively in sport associations, unions and federations can be either volunteers or professionals.

500. The administrators in most of the sport associations are volunteers who act as Board of Administration members or as amateur team managers. They are subject to the limitations and impediments for the participation of individuals in sport institutions (associations, unions, federations) set in Article 3 of law 2725/1999, and they may not be considered as under contract with them.

501. On the contrary, the administration of the TAA and the AAEs is basically entrusted to professional managers, many of whom have had special studies in sport management. They are connected to those sport institutions with a contract, either a dependent labour contract or an independent services contract.

502. In the sports unions and sports federations, the administration is done partly by volunteers and partly by professional managers.

§4. Agents' Regulations

503. According to Article 90, paragraph 5 of law 2725/1999, a decision of the Minister of Sport, following an introduction of the relevant sport federation, the relevant professional league and the relevant unionist instruments of professional athletes and coaches, defines the terms and conditions for the exercise of the profession of those intervening in the signing of contracts between professional athletes or paid athletes or coaches and AAEs or TAA (players' agents).

504. They must possess a licence issued after being subject to examination and can act individually or under partnership only in the sports for which they have got this licence. In their activity, the CC provisions for agency contracts apply.

505. Following the above provision, the Ministerial Decree 237/2002 was issued containing details for agents. They are called mediators of sports contracts (managers or agents), and they are defined as the natural persons who mediate in the drawing up of contracts for the provision of sports services between professional athletes, paid athletes or coaches and sports limited liability companies (AAE) and/or departments of paid athletes (TAA) and gather the conditions of the Decree. Their activity is considered professional activity, and they are connected with their clients with independent services contracts. They are registered in the General Secretariat of Sport upon submitting the necessary documents and passing the exams organized by a Committee of the GGA. In practice, this procedure was not fully applied.

506. Especially in football, FIFA changed its approach twice during the last decade. First, it abolished the old Agents Regulations and left the whole issue in the hands of the national federations who for a long time only registered anyone applying, and in 2023, put into force the new Agent's Regulations which include very strict provisions to control their activity including cap in their fees causing the unionist associations of agents in various countries to claim the cancellation of whole or part of these regulations successfully so far in Germany, Netherlands and England. EPO has already introduced a national agent's regulation in the frame of FIFA, but it is difficult to predict if it will be applied.

§5. Employment and Economic Dispute Settlements

507. The employment and economic disputes of the paid and professional athletes and coaches arising from their contracts are dealt with by the first-degree Committees for the Settlement of Economic Disputes which function within the gulfs of the relevant professional league for basketball and volleyball and EPO for football, while the second-degree ones, which for football is the Football Arbitration Court, in the relevant sport federation.

508. While for basketball and volleyball, the provisions of the CC and Code of Civil Procedure (CPolD) apply, together with the provisions of the Regulation of Article 87 of law 2725/1999, HFF has adapted three regulations applicable in the settlement of the economic Disputes between players and coaches with clubs: The Regulation on the Status and Transfer of Players, the Procedural Regulation of the First-Instance Committee for the Settlement of Economic Disputes and the Procedural Regulation for the Football Arbitration Court. The above committees for football are also competent for the disputes arising from the contracts of player's agents.

§6. Social Security

509. The securing of the athletes' health is a very important issue, and it constitutes a necessary condition for their registration and their participation in training and in games. Therefore, the certification of the athletes' good state of health is compulsory, according to Article 33, paragraph 9 of law 2725/1999, as amended several times. The law provides the issuance of a Health' Card to athletes after a series of medical examinations, where the certification is valid for one year.

510. For the securing of the health of amateur athletes, who are not secured in some insurance institution, either private or public, there is a free hospital treatment, according to Article 36, paragraph 4. For amateur ex-athletes who are not secured and for the support of poor families of deceased athletes, a special account has been created in the General Secretariat of Sports, according to the provisions of Article 36, paragraph 1 of law 2725/1999.

511. The amateur athletes of men and women team sports associations participating in national divisions who sign contracts according to Article 33, paragraph 2 with their associations, the law provides that they are covered by insurance only for the risk of an accident by paying a minimum contribution of 1%. In the event that, during the above insurance, the athlete is not covered for sickness benefits in kind, directly or indirectly, by another insurance, the above persons are also subject to the insurance of the State for this risk. The insurance contributions provided for this case are borne by the insured and his counterparty according to the applicable ratio.

512. The Paid athletes, as well as professional athletes, are covered by the insurance of the branches of the National Social Security Agency (Ethnikos Foreas Koinonikis Asfalisis – EFKA) which replaced the Social Insurance Foundation (I.K.A.). Contributions are calculated exclusively on the basis of the athletes' regular monthly salaries.

513. Non-regular salaries and extraordinary benefits (premium), the amount of which is freely determined upon signing the contract or before the start of the respective leagues of each season, are not subject to contributions.

514. Today, the EFKA contribution rates for pension are 11.32% for employees and 17.99% for employers.

515. Especially for medical care, instead of the Health sector of the EFKA., the athletes of AAEs can be insured by private insurance companies, and the AAE are responsible for paying the insurance premiums by two-thirds and the athletes by one-third. For the terms of the insurance, the relevant professional associations, jointly with the relevant associations of paid athletes, negotiate with the private insurance companies. Exemption from insurance in the health sector of the EFKA occurs only at the time of taking out private insurance.

516. Article 89 also provides that athletes, Members of athletes associations may establish mutual funds, legal entities under private law in accordance with what is defined by the provisions applicable to mutual funds.

517. The amateur athletes who participate in professional championships are also provided with private insurance coverage for their medical care in accordance with the above

§7. Tax Law

518. Amateur athletes whose competitive activity does not constitute professional sports activity do not receive fees, so there is no subject of taxation.

519. For the reimbursement of travel, accommodation and food expenses paid by amateur athletes, an Expense Reimbursement Statement is drawn up to be entered in the books of the Association so that the payment of the expense is recognized for tax purposes in accordance with Article 22 of Law 4172/2013, attaching the corresponding original documents from the tickets, food receipts, hotels, etc., expenses.

520. Amateur athletes though participating in team sports associations of national divisions who have signed contracts with their associations according to Article 33, paragraph 2 of Law 2725/1999 and receive fees, are taxed just like professional athletes.

521. Paid and professional athletes, coaches and other employees of the AAEs and TAA, as well as coaches and other employees of sport associations, pay regular taxation. Their income is taxed as income from salaried services in accordance with paragraph 1 of Article 15 of Law 4172/2013, as well as the tax reductions of Article 16 of the same law as long as the amounts they receive in one-off or instalments do not exceed EUR 40,000 per year.

522. According to POL 1072/2015, a 20% tax is withheld on this amount without exhausting the tax liability of the beneficiaries for these incomes.

523. The tax scale Article 15 of law 4172/2013 is as follows: For income (Salaries, Pensions, Business Activity) EUR 0–10,000 tax rate 9%. For income EUR 10,001–20,000, 22%. For income EUR 20,001–30,000, 28%. For income EUR 30,001–40,000, 36%.

524. According to Article 16 of Law 4172/2013, the tax resulting from the application of Article 15 is reduced depending on the family status of the taxpayer and the number of children dependent on him/her.

525. When the income exceeds EUR 40,000 within the relevant tax year, this total income, including the income up to EUR 40,000, is fully taxable at a tax rate of 22% with the exhaustion of the tax liability, without applying in this case the tax reductions of Article 16 of Law 4172/2013.

Part III. Doping and Sport

Chapter 1. General Issues

526. One of the most important and definitely the most controversial modern problems in the field of sport is the issue of doping. It is a problem difficult to resolve, caused by the use of prohibited substances and methods aiming at the amelioration of the sport performance.[29] Doping actually constitutes a serious sport crime since it falsifies the results of the sport events, and it has side effects on athletes' health with serious social and political dimensions.

527. A lot of efforts have been made in the past for the definition of doping, but a more practical approach made by the World Anti-Doping Code (amended version 2021) seems to have solved this problem. According to Article 1 of the Code, doping is defined as the occurrence of one or more of the anti-doping rule violations set forth in Article 2.1 through Article 2.11 of the Code, which are at present:

- The presence of a prohibited substance or its metabolites or markers in an athlete's sample (Article 2.1).
- The use or attempted use by an athlete of a prohibited substance or a prohibited method (Article 2.2).
- Evading, refusing or failing to submit to sample collection by an athlete (Article 2.3).
- Whereabouts failures by an athlete (Article 2.4).
- Tampering or attempted tampering with any part of doping control by an athlete or other person (Article 2.5).
- The possession of a prohibited substance or a prohibited method by an athlete or athlete support person (Article 2.6).
- Trafficking or attempted trafficking in any prohibited substance or prohibited method by an athlete or other person (Article 2.7).
- The administration or attempted administration by an athlete or other person to any athlete in competition of any prohibited substance or prohibited method or administration or attempted administration to any athlete out of competition of any prohibited substance or prohibited method that is prohibited out of competition (Article 2.8).
- Complicity or attempted complicity by an athlete or other person (Article 2.9).
- Prohibited association by an athlete or other person (Article 2.10).

29. Elements are taken from the work of A. Mavromatis, *Sport Crimes*, 2006, 231, etc.

– Acts by an athlete or other person to discourage or retaliate against reporting to authorities (Article 2.11).

528. The definition of the Greek law 2725/1999, as it was introduced by the law 3057/2002 before the final formulation of the World Anti-Doping Code, is the following: 'Doping is the giving to an athlete or the use by him of a prohibited means (substance or method), as well as the existence in his/her body of a prohibited means or of evidence of the use of such a means' (Article 128B). This definition does not correspond to the definition of the World Anti-Doping Code 2021, which is rendered in Greek by law 4791/2021, but Article 128B has never been removed, so it formally remains in force.

529. Doping is not a modern phenomenon. There are reports from Greek antiquity that some athletes used to go on special diets with certain kinds of meat or dried figs, while in the third century B.C., athletes used to eat some special species of mushrooms to improve their performance. In the modern era, doping appeared at the end of the nineteenth century and expanded at the end of the twentieth.

530. The most important reason that leads athletes to use illicit means and methods for the improvement of their performance is the inborn and continuous human tendency towards the best as well as the competition, which constitutes a substantial element of the sport activity. Nowadays, the main causes and reasons for the spreading of the doping phenomenon can be found:

– In the syndrome of medicines. The rapid development of the medicine industry ceaselessly feeds both the sport and social field with numerous medicines. For example, students and workers resort to using vitamins in order to copy with the needs of their studies or their work. This is the case for the athletes, too. Nowadays, athletes have many pharmaceutical choices for the improvement of their sport performance.
– In the commercialization of sport. Nowadays, the sport activity has acquired an intense economic dimension. The sport teams are great businesses for the function of which enormous capitals are required, as vast amounts of money are necessary for the organization of international importance. The public allocations cannot cover these amounts of money, so the money of the sponsors or other private institutions is indispensable. All these sponsors or private institutions invest in sports only if they expect an augmentation of their profits, which can take place through the advertisement of their products. What is more, the advertisement has the best results only if a lot of people watch it, which may happen if the game is interesting, i.e., if great sport performances occur during this game. These great performances can be more easily achieved with the use of doping substances.
– In the pursuing of glory, of a bonus or of a good contract as the aftermath of the victory or the record. An olive branch and a laurel crown were bestowed to the winners of the Olympic Games in antiquity. Their own reward was their recognition in the cities of their origin. Nowadays, the winner wins much more. First, the great publicity offers glory and fame to the champion, to the Olympic champion or to a record holder. Simultaneously, the winners of a serious game or those

who achieve a record earn a considerable bonus from their sponsor, from their team or even from the authorities of their country. Finally, the victory or the record guarantees a contract with a team or a sponsor with better terms, conditions and clauses. All these benefits coming with the victory push the athletes to the use of prohibited means and methods to acquire them.
- In the multiplication and the increase of the level of difficulty of the sport events and the increase of obligations of the athletes on an annual basis.
- In the incapability of the legislation to control the production, import, trade and sale of prohibited substances that may cause damage to the athletes' health and to the lack of information for these damages and dangers.
- In the political ambitions or in the nationalism of some politicians. It is highly likely that some politicians or other people of high authority tolerate, cover, or even favour the use of doping substances so that they receive the benefit of some international success of their athletes.
- In the need of the athlete to maintain the same level of performance at the end of his career or to compete despite an injury or even to fix his weight to participate in a game.
- In other factors that are not related to the sport activities, like the factors that urge young people to taste drugs (to confront their excessive stress, etc.).

531. Doping is considered a major problem, especially because of its consequences to the health of athletes, to sport itself as well as social ones:

- Consequences to the health of the athletes. The damages caused by substances or methods of doping to the health of the athletes are various, appearing directly or in the long-term and sometimes leading to death. These damages can be daily problems (insomnias, overreactions, temporary effects on the heart system, etc.) or even more serious problems, such as serious heart problems, breath problems, cancers, etc. Some of these substances may also cause addiction.
- Consequences to the sport. The main consequence of doping in the sport field is the inequality caused among the participants in the game. This inequality actually alters or falsifies the game result. This way, fair play as an expression of the sport spirit and the Olympic ideal is violated. The alteration of the game result nowadays brings about serious financial side effects since it causes a different distribution of the property dependent on it directly (bonuses, other financial profits, etc.) or indirectly (sponsorship contracts, advertisements, broadcasting exclusive rights, etc.).
- Social consequences. There are further consequences of the doping phenomenon, which have a more social dimension, such as (i) the spreading of doping for reasons of indirect compulsion since usually the athletes are obliged to resort to the use of doping substances and methods without their proper will, in order to be able to compete with the doped co-athletes, (ii) the bad example for the young people, which is expressed with their willingness to overlook the dangers of the use of prohibited substances, if they could achieve great performances with the help of these substances, (iii) the identification of sport with these practices, a reality that becomes a part of the social conscience and finally leads to the

degrading of the meaning of sport as a social and cultural good and as an educational tool, and (iv) the collapse of the myth of athletes that constitute ideals for young people and they finally turn out to become bad models.

Chapter 2. Public Regulation

532. All international sport institutions, as it is normal, have dealt with the doping phenomenon. Under the initiative of the IOC, the WADA was founded as a foundation according to the Swiss law. WADA, governed by representatives of major international sport institutions as well as representatives of public authorities from all over the world has undertaken since the beginning of the twenty-first century the major responsibility in the fight against doping at the sporting level worldwide. The World Anti-Doping Code, formulated and accepted at the World Anti-Doping Congress in Copenhagen in 2003, has already been amended four times – last in 2021 – is the basic instrument of harmonization and globalization of the fight against doping.

533. The European Convention against doping prepared by the Council of Europe and ratified by almost all European countries has been one of the most serious international elements of coordination of the international fight against doping in sport. Another international convention against doping was adopted at the end of 2005 under UNESCO in order to coordinate at a global level the common fight of governments and public authorities of the world.

534. Greece is one of the first countries to acquire relevant legal coverage against doping. In 1975, law 75/75 (Articles 58 and 59) set out penal and disciplinary sanctions for the crime of doping. A few years later, law 1646/1986 (Articles 7–11) modified the relevant provisions by maintaining the penal and disciplinary dimension of this issue. In 1996, Greece ratified the European Convention against doping (law 2371/1996) and on 31 December 2006, the UNESCO International Convention against doping in sport (Law 3516/2006).

535. During the recent international discussion about doping at the beginning of the century, law 3057/2002 added in law 2725/1999 a whole chapter (Article 128A–128ID), which replaced law 1646/1986 and is formally still in force, even though amended several times (laws 3708/2008, 4049/2012, 4446/2016 and 4726/2020). Although it was formulated before the final text of the World Anti-Doping Code, the Greek law is very severe and in the same direction as the Code regulations, including preventive as well as restraining measures and sanctions.

536. Law 4373/2016 introduced necessary amendments in the legislation against doping in order to harmonize with the amended World Anti-Doping Code 2015, cancelling all previous contrary provisions.

537. In 2021, law 4791/2021 became the main anti-doping law in Greece to incorporate the amended World Anti-Doping Code 2021 but has already been amended twice with laws 4825/2021 and 4831/2021 following pressure from WADA to correspond in every detail to the provisions of the Code.

538. Most of the prescribed anti-doping provisions in the sports law (e.g., definitions, prohibited means, doping control procedures, doping disciplinary violations, disciplinary sanctions) have now been regulated in a detailed and specific manner by law, 4791/2021, so that their existence or even their parallel application is no longer of practical importance, while all regulations that make sense to continue to apply should be modernized and harmonized with modern developments in the field of anti-doping and the guidelines indicated by WADA. At the same time, it is necessary to improve the legal and technical aspects of those provisions that remain, as there are terms and procedures that have changed (e.g., the law refers to ESCAN which has been abolished and replaced by EOCAN).

539. The national sport federations must include in their regulations the relevant provisions of the IOC, all of which conform to the principles of the World Anti-Doping Code (Article 26, paragraph 4 in combination with Article 27 of law 2725/1999).

540. At the national level, the highest anti-doping authority is EOKAN, which replaced ESKAN.[30]

541. The substances or methods that cause a technical alteration to the sport performance and harm the health of the athletes are mentioned in principle according to the sports law and in a special decision of the Ministers of Sport and Health, which was issued every year (Article 128C, paragraph 2 of law 2725/1999), compatible with the yearly updated Prohibited List of WADA.

542. Article 4 of law 4791/2021, corresponding to Article 4 of the World Anti-Doping Code, provides that the Prohibited List, as published and revised from time to time by WADA and described in Article 4.1. of the Code, is an integral part of the law. Unless otherwise provided in the Prohibited List or a revision thereof, the Prohibited List and its revisions shall become effective under these Anti-Doping Rules three months after publication by WADA without any further action. All athletes and third parties are bound by the prohibited list and any revision thereof, from the date they come into force, without any further formality. It is the responsibility of all athletes and third parties to familiarize themselves with the updated version of the prohibited list and all revisions thereof.

543. The Prohibited List sets out the Prohibited Substances and Prohibited Methods which are prohibited, at all times (both in-competition an out-of-competition) as doping because of their potential to enhance performance in future competitions or their potential for concealment and those the substances and methods prohibited only in competition.

544. It is worth mentioning that it is indispensably connected to doping as an offence the previous existence of a regulation prohibiting the use of the substance detected in the athlete's body specimen. In other words, the prohibited substance is

30. *See* above paras 39 et seq.

not any substance that may have enhanced the athlete's performance or caused him/her a body damage, but only a substance that is included in the valid Prohibited List. A substance not included in the valid Prohibited List when the doping control takes place may under no circumstances cause a sanction to the athlete, even if it enhances his/her performance and risks his health.

545. On the contrary, it is not possible for an athlete to maintain the result he/she achieved in a competition where he/she participated having used a prohibited substance, even if he/she proves that this did not affect his performance and may not cause any damage to his/her health, because in any case he/she has participated in that competition by violating the rules that govern it.

546. An athlete is entitled to use some prohibited substances for purely medical reasons if he/she fulfils the necessary conditions to be granted a Therapeutic Use Exemption according to Article 4.4 of the Code and the International Standard of WADA. Since the Greek law was formulated before the Code, it contained different provisions in Article 128Z, paragraph 5 and Article 4, paragraph 4 of the Law 4791/2021 introduced the provisions of the Code.

547. According to the sport law, doping control is carried out for the athletes of the sports of the sport federations having the special sport recognition for the securing of the genuineness of the sport effort and of the sport result and for the securing of the athletes' health (paragraph 1 of Article 128D of law 2725/1999, added with Article 55 of law 3057/2002). The athletes are obliged to be subject to doping control whenever asked to do so by the competent according to the law instruments, which may be international, such as WADA, IOC or the relevant international federation or national, such as EOKAN. Article 5 of the law 4791/2021 introduced the provisions of the Code for the controls and investigations.

548. The doping control is carried out by the competent sample collection personnel registered in the Registry of the sample control personnel of EOKAN, according to PD 87/2020. Doping controls must be realized in a way that ensures the equal treatment of the athletes (Article 128D, paragraph 8) and respect for their personalities. The valid legislation for the protection of the person and of the personal data of the athlete must be secured according to paragraph 5 of Article 128I of law 2725/1999.

549. According to Article 5 of law 4791/2021, which introduced the provisions of Article 5 of the Code, the procedure of doping control is the one described in the International Standard for Testing and Investigations (ISTI) of WADA. The doping control procedure contains:

- The reception of samples, according to the ISTI Guidelines for Sample Collection of WADA.

– The analysis of the samples on the basis of generally accepted rules of science and in recognized laboratories. The sample analysis is carried out by a WADA-accredited Doping Control Laboratory[31] according to the provisions of the International Standard for Laboratories of WADA.

550. Sport law provides that doping control is obligatory during the matches of all professional leagues and the Cup of Greece, in which AAEs or TAA participate, that is to say, in the highest divisions of football, basketball and volleyball men's championships (Article 128E, paragraph 2) and must be carried out in at least one match per championship per competition day (Article 128E, paragraph 3). In the games of the supreme amateur division of the same sports, as well as in the highest division of nonprofessional team sports, doping control is obligatory in at least six matches of the regular season and one match per competition day in the playoff round (Article 128E, paragraph 4). The number of athletes per team to be controlled is usually two according to the regulations of the relevant federation but can be higher upon the decision of EOKAN. The procedure for the drawing of lots among the athletes of the teams in order to draw those who will be tested is described in the regulations of each sport. In individual sports, doping control takes place necessarily on at least one competition day of the national championships of the supreme age category (Article 128E, paragraph 5).

551. In practice, this no longer applies systematically even though the law is still in force because the current trend worldwide is to focus on out-of-competition testing.

552. According to Article 5 of the law 4791/2021 corresponding to Article 5 of the Code, the National Anti-Doping Organization has the authority to control all athletes, in-competition and out-of-competition. The National Anti-Doping Agency may require any athlete over whom it has jurisdiction to control, including any athlete serving a period of ineligibility, to provide a sample at anytime and anywhere. WADA has in-competition and out-of-competition control jurisdiction as provided in Article 20.7.10. of the Code as well.

553. In international events held in Greece, the international organization responsible for the event has the authority to conduct control. In national events held in Greece, the National Anti-Doping Agency has the authority to conduct control.

554. The National Anti-Doping Agency compiles a list of controlled athletes who are required to provide tracking information, as provided for in the International Standard for Testing and Investigations and are subject to the consequences for violations of Article 2.4. In accordance with the International Standard for Testing and Investigations, an athlete included on the Controlled Athlete List shall: (a)

31. In Greece, there was an accredited Doping Control Laboratory seated in the Athens Olympic Sport Center, which lost its accreditation and currently all samples are sent to laboratories abroad.

provide the National Anti-Doping Agency with their tracking information on a quarterly basis, (b) update this information as necessary so that remain accurate and complete at all times, and (c) remain available for review, consistent with its tracking information.

555. Results management takes place according to the provisions of Articles 7 and 8 of law 4791/2021 and the Code. Doping as Criminal Offence.

556. Greece is one of the countries, where doping constitutes since 1975 a special crime in addition to the possibility that committing it may also be considered as committing some other crime of the PC or special penal laws, such as body damages and or crimes connected with drugs.

557. The difference between the Greek approach and the more common international one is that in Greece, even the athlete who uses prohibited substances or methods commits a crime. This means that Greek law's main intention is not to protect the athlete's health – this would be an unacceptable interpretation because self-injury is not a crime in principle in Greece – which is well protected from the provision about the body damage, but the result of the sport events from being falsified by the participation of some athletes against the rules.

558. The main doping crime as set out in Article 128Θ, paragraph 1 of the law 2725/1999 is the administration to an athlete of a natural or chemical substance or biological or biotechnological material or the application on him/her of a method among those prohibited by the relevant common ministerial decision (which is issued according to Article 128Γ of law 2725/1999), which contains the valid prohibited list. The purpose of the person who commits this crime shall be to improve the athlete's performance and ability during or in view of his/her participation in sports events. Therefore, the crime is not committed by a doctor who administers a medicine to an athlete for medical reasons, although in this case, if the Therapeutic Use Exemption procedure is not followed, the doctor may have committed a disciplinary offence. There is no need for the athlete to have used the substance or method in order for the crime to be committed.

559. The crime is punished with an imprisonment of three up to five years plus a fine unless the same action is punished more severely by another penal provision, for example, if the substance is included in the list of prohibited drugs, the administration of which is punished with more severe penalties as a felony. Apart from the imprisonment, the court inflicts on the condemned person the prohibition to exercise any profession related to sport for another period equal to the imprisonment as an additional penalty.

560. Imprisonment of five up to ten years is imposed, if the culprit commits the above acts either professionally or with the aim of providing himself or another with a financial benefit, if the act is not punished more heavily according to another provision.

561. If the athlete is of minor age (under 18 years old), the crime is considered a felony and is punished by imprisonment of at least ten years as well as with the deprivation of the right of the condemned person to exercise any profession related to sport for life regardless of the imprisonment period imposed.

562. As already mentioned, the use by an athlete of a natural or chemical substance or biological or biotechnological material or the permission of the application on him/her of a method among those prohibited by the relevant common ministerial decision is considered as crime as well (Article 128Θ, paragraph 2). The purpose of the athlete must be to improve his/her performance and ability during or in view of his/her participation in sports events. Therefore, the crime is not committed by an athlete who uses a prohibited substance for medical reasons, although in this case, if the Therapeutic Use Exemption procedure is not followed, the athlete has committed a disciplinary offence. This crime is punished with imprisonment of two to five years unless the same action is punished more severely by another penal provision.

563. The possession by an athlete of a substance or material as above that has not been legally registered in his health card is punishable by a fine of at least EUR 5,000 if the act is not punished more heavily according to another provision.

564. Another doping crime, which was only recently standardized, is the one described in paragraph 4 of Article 128Θ. According to this provision whoever creates, produces, inserts, modifies, stores, transports, imports, exports, trades, sells, buys, possesses, offers or finances the purchase of the prohibited substances and methods included in the relevant common ministerial decision with the aim to improve any athlete's performance and ability during or in view of his/her participation in sports events, is punished with imprisonment of three up to five years plus fine, unless the same action is punished more severely by another penal provision, for example, if the substance is included in the list of the prohibited drugs. If the perpetrator commits these acts in sports facilities or with the aim of administering substances or applying methods to minor athletes, imprisonment of at least ten years as well as deprivation of the right of the condemned person to exercise any profession related to sport for life regardless of the imprisonment period shall be imposed.

565. Final penal provision is in paragraph 6, according to which whoever prevents the competent authorities from carrying out a doping control, or whoever destroys or alters the samples or forges or alters the doping results, is sentenced to imprisonment of two to five years. In the event that these acts are committed intentionally by a doping sampler within the meaning of this law, a member of the staff of EOKAN shall be punished with imprisonment of five to ten years.

566. In Article 128IΔ of the law, some penal crimes related to horse doping are foreseen as following: whoever supplies any method or electroshock to a horse, prohibited by the list of the Code of Horse Races in order to stipulate or to hinder its physical abilities or to artificially alter its physical performance, is sentenced to two to five years imprisonment plus fine (Article 128IΔ, paragraph 1). The same penalty is set out for whoever possesses such substances with the aim of supplying them to horses (Article 128IΔ, paragraph 2). A penalty of imprisonment of two to five years is set out for whoever denies the sample taking, hinders the doping control or submits false data of control (Article 128IΔ, paragraph 4). If the jockey is found under the influence of a prohibited substance during doping control, he is sentenced to two to five years imprisonment unless the same act is punished heavily by another provision (Article 129IΔ, paragraph 3).

Chapter 3. Private Regulation – Doping as Disciplinary Offence

567. Article 128Z contained provisions for the confrontation of doping as a disciplinary offence but should be considered cancelled since Articles 10–12 of law 4791/2021 have incorporated the provisions of the World Anti-Doping Code, and those should apply.

568. According to the World Anti-Doping Code, any anti-doping rule violation among those described in Article 2.1–2.11 constitutes a disciplinary offence.

569. Violation of an anti-doping rule in individual sports, in the context of in-competition control, leads automatically to the cancellation of the results achieved in the specific competition and in all subsequent competitions, including the removal of medals, grades and awards (Article 9 of law 4791/2021 and the Code). This application of the strict liability rule, although it seems unfair in some cases, is necessary considering the nature of doping as a violation of rules governing the sport competitions as already described. It is though contradictive not to accept the same principle in team sports (Article 11 of the Code).

570. According to Article 10 of law 4791/2021 and the Code, an anti-doping rule violation during or in connection with a sporting event may, at the decision of the governing body of the sporting event, result in the cancellation of all individual results of the athlete achieved in that sporting event, together with all consequences, including removal of all medals, points and awards. Factors considered in determining whether to invalidate other results in a sporting event may include, in particular, the seriousness of the athlete's anti-doping rule violation and whether the athlete has tested negative in other events. If the Athlete establishes that he is not at fault for the violation, his individual results in the other Competitions shall not be annulled unless such results in other Competitions than the one in which the anti-doping rule violation was committed are likely to have been affected by the violation thereof. The period of exclusion imposed for violation of Article 2.1., 2.2. or 2.6. is four years unless the athlete or another person can demonstrate that the anti-doping rule violation was not intentional. In such cases, the exclusion period lasts for two years. If the athlete can prove that any intake or use occurred outside of competition and was not related to athletic performance, then the period of ineligibility is three months. In addition, the period of Ineligibility calculated hereunder may be reduced to one month if the Athlete or other person satisfactorily completes a substance abuse rehabilitation program approved by the National Anti-Doping Agency.

571. The period of Ineligibility for anti-doping rule violations of Article 2.3. or 2.5. shall be set at four years unless: (i) in the case of failure to submit a Sample, the Athlete can demonstrate that the commission of an anti-doping rule violation was not intentional, in which case the period of Ineligibility shall be set at two years, (ii) in all other cases, the athlete or other person can demonstrate special circumstances justifying a reduction of the period of ineligibility, in which case such period shall vary from two to four years depending on the degree of culpability of the athlete or other person, or (iii) in the event that a protected person or athlete is involved, then the imposed consequence is, at a minimum, a reprimand without a period of ineligibility and, at a maximum, two years of ineligibility, depending on the degree of culpability of the protected person or the victim.

572. For violations of Article 2.4., the exclusion period is two years, with the possibility of reduction to a minimum of one year, depending on the degree of culpability of the athlete. The flexibility between two years and one year ineligibility in this article shall not apply to athletes with repeated conduct of changing tracking information at the last minute or other conduct that raises serious suspicion that the athlete is attempting to avoid being available for testing.

573. For violations of Article 2.7. or 2.8., the period of disqualification ranges from at least four years to lifetime disqualification, depending on the seriousness of the violation. Violation of Article 2.7. or 2.8. concerning a protected person is considered a particularly serious offence and, if committed by athlete support personnel for offences other than the substances of special reference, results in a lifetime ban for the athlete support personnel. In addition, significant violations of Article 2.7. or 2.8. which may also violate non-sporting laws and regulations, must be reported to the appropriate administrative, professional or judicial authorities.

574. For violations of Article 2.9., the imposed exclusion period ranges from at least two years to lifetime exclusion, depending on the severity of the violation.

575. For violations of Article 2.10., the exclusion period is two years, with the possibility of reduction to a minimum of one year, depending on the degree of culpability of the athlete or other person and the other circumstances of the case.

576. For violations of Article 2.11., the period of disqualification ranges from at least two years to lifetime disqualification, depending on the seriousness of the violation by the athlete or the other person.

577. If the National Anti-Doping Agency finds in an individual case that it involves an anti-doping rule violation, other than violations of Articles 2.7. (trafficking or attempted trafficking), 2.8. (administration or attempted administration), 2.9. (collusion or attempted collusion) or 2.11. (actions of an athlete or other person to discourage or retaliate against reporting), that there are aggravating circumstances that justify the imposition of a period of ineligibility longer than the prescribed sanction, then the period of ineligibility, which is otherwise enforceable, shall be increased to two years, depending on the seriousness of the offence and the nature of the aggravating circumstances, unless the athlete or another person can prove that he did not knowingly commit the Anti-Doping Rule violation.

578. If an athlete or other person proves in a specific case that he is not at fault, then the otherwise applicable period of exclusion is eliminated.

579. The otherwise applicable period of exclusion may be reduced, based on the degree of culpability of the athlete or other person, up to half of the exclusion period that would otherwise be imposed. If the otherwise enforceable period of disqualification is for life, the reduced period hereunder may not be less than eight years.

580. The National Anti-Doping Agency may, before a decision on appeal, suspend a portion of the consequences, other than disqualification and mandatory disclosure, imposed in a particular case if the Athlete or other Person provided material assistance to an anti-doping organization.

581. When an Athlete or other Person, after being notified by the National Anti-Doping Organization of a possible anti-doping rule violation that would result in a period of ineligibility of four years or more, admits to the violation and accepts the imposition of the period of ineligibility no later than twenty days after receiving the relevant notification, the athlete or other person may receive a one year reduction in the period of ineligibility imposed by the National Anti-Doping Agency.

582. In the event of a second anti-doping rule violation by an Athlete or other Person, the period of Ineligibility shall be the greater of: (a) a period of Ineligibility of six months, or (b) a period of Ineligibility between: (i) the sum of the Ineligible Periods, which imposed for the first anti-doping rule violation and the period of Ineligibility otherwise imposed for the second anti-doping rule violation as it would have been if it had been a first violation, and (ii) twice the period of Ineligibility otherwise imposed for the second anti-doping rule violation; as it would be treated if it were a first offence. The period of exclusion within this range is determined, taking into account the totality of the circumstances and the degree of culpability of the athlete or other person in relation to the second offence. The third anti-doping rule violation results in a lifetime ineligibility unless the third violation qualifies for elimination or reduction of the period of ineligibility under Article 10.5 or 10.6 or involves a violation of Article 2.4. In these cases, the disqualification period is from eight years to lifetime disqualification.

583. After the Sample or Anti-Doping Rule Violation In addition to the automatic disqualification of results in the competition in which the positive sample was detected in accordance with Article 9, all other competitive results of the Athlete recorded since the date of collection of a positive sample, whether in-competition or out-of-competition or other anti-doping rule violation committed, until the beginning of any period of provisional suspension (provisional ineligibility) or disqualification are void unless otherwise ordered by the authorities of justice, while all prescribed consequences are imposed; such as the loss of medals, points and awards.

584. According to Article 11 of law 4791/2021 and the World Anti-Doping Code, when more than one member of a sports team in a team sport has been notified of an anti-doping rule violation, in the context of a sports event, the Controlling Body of the sporting event conducts targeted checks on the team during the sporting event. If more than two members of an athletic team in a team sport are found to have committed an anti-doping rule violation during an athletic event, the governing body of that athletic event shall impose the appropriate sanction on the team (e.g., deduction of points, disqualification from competition or sporting event, or other sanction), in addition to any consequences imposed on individual Athletes who have committed an anti-doping rule violation.

Chapter 4. Competent Judicial Body

585. The law provision that the relevant sport federation or professional league is obliged to forward the case to its competent judicial instrument (Article 128I, paragraph 3) should be considered cancelled because Article 8 of law 4791/2021 in line with Article 8 of the Code includes a provision that the National Anti-Doping Agency shall establish a hearing panel (first-degree disciplinary panel) which shall have jurisdiction to hear and determine whether an Athlete or other Person subject hereto has committed an anti-doping rule violation and, where applicable, to impose penalties.

586. The primary disciplinary committee of the National Anti-Doping Agency consists of an independent chairman and eight independent members. Each member is appointed after taking into account their required experience in anti-doping matters, including their legal, athletic, medical and/or scientific experience. Each member is appointed for a term of three years, which may be renewed once. The first-instance disciplinary committee conducts the hearing and makes decisions without interference from the National Anti-Doping Agency or any third party.

587. Article 13 of law 4791/2021 introduced a provision for the appeals harmonized with the Code. Appeals may be submitted to ASEAD or CAS depending on whether the athletes or the competitions are at the national or international level. It has to be accepted though that appeals related to football should be addressed to the EPO Appeal Committee.

588. There is one more kind of doping offence, horse doping, which is sanctioned following the provisions of the regulations of the International Equestrian Federation and the Code of Horse Races.

Part IV. Sport and Commerce

Chapter 1. General Issues – Challenges

589. Society and people's lives have changed rapidly during the last decades, and inevitably, this has affected sporting activity. The boost came with the transmission of sporting events on television and later on through the internet. Exclusive rights for advertisements through athletes and teams are disposed of at increasingly higher prices. The desire of international sports institutions to find capital for the support of their activities has led to the commercialization of sport. Media and television rights, sponsoring and merchandising, along with the income from tickets and the transfer of athletes, have become the main source of income for the sports companies in professional sports. The cost of the exclusive broadcasting of major sport events has dramatically increased worldwide. The exclusiveness of a right to broadcast a sport event has developed along with the appearance of the financial activity in the field of sports, especially after the gigantism of the Olympic Games and other major events and the great interest of the world's population to watch them. The professionalism in many sports and the financial activity connected to it has made many countries introduce laws for the exclusive broadcasting of sport events.

590. One of the biggest challenges the sports industry faces today is keeping up with the pace of technological advancements. Many fans connect with their favourite teams through social media, which puts pressure on teams to constantly keep updating their Facebook timelines and Twitter feeds. Likewise, venues must also keep up with the pace. Not having Wi-Fi can be a major turn-off for fans who want to stay connected throughout the game. Thus, if teams are not proactive with social media and do not have the capability to entice fans with modern technology, fans will simply not follow them or go to games in person.

591. Implementing new technologies can be expensive. Virtual reality, advanced analytics, and stadium enhancements are costly endeavours. Sports organizations with limited financial resources may fall behind on the latest cutting-edge technologies. These new technologies can also disrupt the traditional revenue models for sports organizations, affecting ticket sales and broadcasting rights.

592. The sports industry also faces the challenge of finding game day experiences that simply cannot be experienced at home. This includes:

– pregame shows;
– in-game entertainment (kiss cam, chants, etc.);
– halftime entertainment;
– postgame celebrations.

593. With the rise in ticket prices, fans have higher expectations on game day. Stadiums with excessive post-game exit congestion or inadequate facilities can be a turn-off for fans, forcing them to go elsewhere.

594. During these modern activities, data privacy and compliance with the respective laws raise limits that must be respected. As sports marketers collect and analyse fan data for targeted campaigns, they must remain in compliance with data privacy regulations. Protecting fan information is crucial, and privacy laws like the General Data Protection Regulation applied in Greece with the law 4624/2019 add complexity to data management.

Chapter 2. Public Regulation

§1. Media and Television Rights

595. The broadcast and telecast of sport events constitute a problem that needs research within the field of the sport law.[32]

596. This is a property and not a moral, intellectual property right. Thus – that is, regarding the possibility of the additional application of the provisions of Law 2121/93 (about the characteristics of broadcast licences, the duration of the right, etc.) – the general question of the characterization of the sports competition as an intellectual work or not has arisen.[33] The Greek and foreign theory, as well as the jurisprudence of the European Court of Justice (ECJ), approach it negatively without, however, irresistible arguments, such as its connection with the 'business provision' of the stadium, the lack of originality or individuality of the game, the lack of intellectual venture, etc. The violation of this absolute right implies tortious liability according to 914 CC, but also according to 730 CC, but probably also according to AK 904 (if the offender obtained unjustified profit), etc. In any case, the right to matches already held and therefore recorded on a material carrier should be distinguished from the (currently, however) right to the future.[34]

597. In Greece, the right to transmit and distribute games is regulated by the sport law 2725/1999. Special provisions set out the terms and the conditions for the free or paid transmission and telecasting of sport events (Article 84 and 84A of law 2725/1999 as amended), such as: (a) the right to subsidize the exclusive privileges, (b) the free transmission of film extracts, and (c) the paid transmission of sport events.

598. The exploitation of a sport event as a spectacle falls under the commercial activity of the institution – organizer of this sport event. This exploitation contains the right to give the exclusive privilege to a telecasting station to transmit the sport event or to distribute it to news bulletins or to prohibit its transfer. Such a contract between the organizer of a sport event and a telecasting station or channel includes: (a) the concession of the exclusive right, (b) the broad- or telecasting of the game or the sport event, (c) the news bulletin distribution, (d) the prohibition of the further transfer of this privilege, (e) the exclusiveness of the telecasting.

599. According to the law, the abovementioned exclusive right involves the transmission and the news bulletin distribution of the sport event, on condition that the telecasting station to whom this exclusiveness is given is not allowed to exploit further this privilege by transferring it to a third person.

---

32. Elements are taken from the work of K. Christodoulou, *Sports Law*, 2023, 125 et seq. and D. Panagiotopoulos, *Sports Law, Systematic View – Application*, 2005, 523 et seq.
33. K. Christodoulou, *Sports Law*, 2023, 126 et seq. with an interesting approach.
34. K. Christodoulou as above.

600. According to the law (Article 84 of law 2725/1999), every sport association, TAA or AAE has the right to allow on charge the broadcasting or the telecasting of the sport events in which its team is the host team. The sport federations have the same rights as far as the organizations of the national teams and the games for the Cup of Greece are concerned. Furthermore, according to Article 84, paragraph 2 of law 2725/1999, the further transfer of this right is not allowed without the written consent of the association, the federation, etc.

601. Regarding the sports of football and basketball, a certain percentage of the money gained by the sport associations, etc., due to the exploitation of the broadcasting and telecasting rights, is received by the HFF (EPO), the EOK and the professional leagues of these sports according to Article 84, paragraph 8 of law 2725/1999.

602. No licence is required from the associations, the federations, the TAA or the AAEs for the telecasting of extracts of the sport events, on condition that this telecasting serves an informative purpose (Article 84, paragraphs 3 and 6 of law 2725/1999). The broadcasting or telecasting for each day is limited to three dispatches with a maximum duration of three minutes each. Between two dispatches, there must be an intermission of at least one hour.

603. Furthermore, a special list of local, national and international sport organizations of increased interest and importance for the Greek society is created. These organizations have to be transmitted by channels of free and broad reception so that the people's right to information is secured (Article 84, paragraph 7).

604. Article 84A inserted an exception to the rule that the rights belong in principle to the host team for the Super League 2, which is the second division for football, and the law provides the centralized distribution of the media and television rights by the respective professional league and not by the clubs.

605. Needless to say, the rights for international competitions in which Greek teams participate are defined according to the regulations and the provisions of the European or International federation which organizes the competition. For example, UEFA, for its clubs' competitions, defines the clubs as owners of those rights for the qualification rounds but keeps the centralized distribution in the main stages of the competitions.

606. Barring the characterization of the match as an intellectual work, the protection of those who have contributed to its conduct and transmission is still beyond the limits of the powers of Sports Law Legislation Article 84 2725/1999 in the context of, in particular, Article 57 CC (but if additional illegality is proven), Article 904 (if it will be the enrichment of a third party with his own assets and powers), Articles 330 et seq., against third parties and with the terms of Article 914 CC, KPolD 72 or with (on a case-by-case basis only) proportional application of provisions of Law 2121/1993.[35]

35. K. Christodoulou as above.

§2. SPONSORING

607. Sponsoring is a notion of the classical ancient Greek period, one of the most important cultural and social institutions.[36] It was first introduced by Klisthenis at the end of the sixth century B.C., and it flourished during the fifth century B.C. In Panathinea, a great ancient festival, including sport events, one famous sponsor was Herodis the Attic, who undertook and paid for the construction of the marble stadium. The ancient Greek cities recognized the contribution of the sponsors – donators, and they used to inscribe their names on marble slates and honour and pay respect to them.

608. Sponsors in the modern era appeared in the first Olympic Games in Athens (1896), and today, they constitute a major source of income for all international sports institutions.

609. In Greece, the phenomenon of sponsoring started to spread rapidly, mostly in professional sports, football and basketball, but also in some popular amateur sports such as track and field and weightlifting. Nevertheless, there is no explicit legal framework regulating the sponsoring issues. In paragraph 4 of Article 33 of law 2725/1999, it is mentioned that amateur athletes of individual or team sports are allowed to sign contracts of sponsorship or of advertisement of products or services with individuals or legal entities.

610. In professional sport, there is almost no provision regulating the sponsoring contracts. According to the sport law, the AAE is obliged to submit to the EEA every kind of sponsorship contract, advertising company, etc. (Article 77A of law 2725/1999).

611. In the modern sports world, sponsoring can take various forms, such as the financial support of athletes for a certain period of time, the financial support of sporting events, huge sums of money as prizes in case of victories or breaking records (e.g., Golden League of athletics), addition, in the name of the group, the brand name of the company (Title-Sponsoring).

I. Sponsoring Individual Sports Athletes

612. In general, individual sports do not have the same visibility as team sports and their visibility is limited during the Olympic Games period. There are, however, individual sports that have greater visibility, such as athletics, swimming and, to a lesser extent, gymnastics and other sports. It is typical that athletics champions have the reputation of national heroes. That is why the companies interested in entering the sponsoring field could not remain unmoved and not take advantage of the visibility and appeal of these athletes. Thus, large companies have entered the

36. Elements are taken from the work of D. Panagiotopoulos, *Sports Law, Systematic View – Application*, 2005, 533, etc.

field of athletics and other individual sports, concluding sponsorship contracts with the athletes. The sponsoring contracts entered into by individual and team sports athletes must, according to Article 33 paragraph 4 of Law 2725/1999 to be submitted for approval to the relevant sports federation.

II. Sponsoring Sports Teams

613. The visibility of football, basketball, volleyball and other team sports is huge. The groups represent, for a very large part of the population, a kind of religion, causing it very often unfortunately to deviate and exaggerate. Thus, sponsors take advantage of this appeal, concluding sponsorship contracts with sports teams, the content of which may vary. It may be agreed, that is, that the athletes of the association or sports corporation will wear clothes and shoes of the sponsor's company and in the matches in which the insignia and the brand of the company will appear or that there will be banners on the field with the logo and the name of the company or that the team will simply acquire a 'name' by adding to its name, the name of the sponsor's company. Each athlete is bound by the team's decision as long as he/she appears as a member of the team. The team agrees that the athlete will promote the sponsor by wearing certain clothing, and the athlete has the obligation to comply while not having contracted himself. In other words, we have a unique contract against a third party according to the provisions of the CC 415. A question arises as to whether this contract is valid in which one contracting party (sports corporation, sports club) is bound that a third party that has not contracted (athlete) will provide a service that in this case has the character of tolerance of personal insults (very often photos of athletes are used by the sponsors of the clubs in which athletes have the right to the same image). The problem is greater if we take into account that the athletes, in case of non-compliance, will be sanctioned by the respective sports body. The issue appears – and indeed to a greater extent – in relation to the sponsors of the sports federations and the athletes of the federation. Often, a sports federation (for every sport, there is a federation) can conclude a sponsorship contract with a sponsor with the result that all the athletes of the sport of the relevant federation participate in a contract in which they have not contracted. An indicative example is that of the Russian international ski athlete Tsopelova, whose photos were used by the sponsor of the Russian Ski Federation. The question of the protection of athletes from these contracts, therefore, arises. In my opinion, Article AK 415 regarding the conclusion of a contract at the expense of a third party is applicable in principle so that in case of non-fulfilment of the athlete to create an obligation of compensation at the expense of the club or the federation. In the event that photos of athletes have already been used without their consent, Articles of the CC 57 et seq. will be applicable. Now, regarding the possible internal sanctions of the athletes in case of non-compliance, the athletes will be able to request the annulment of the decisions of the collective bodies, which took the decision depending on the legal form of the legal entity. Thus, in case we have a sports club or federation, which is a legal entity under private law, anyone with a legal interest can request the annulment of the decision based on Article AK 10192 due to the opposition to the decision to the law (AK 57, AK 281).

III. Sponsoring Sports Events

614. Sponsoring of sporting events is when a sporting event is financed in exchange for the promotion of the sponsor. Sports events that can be the subject of a sponsorship agreement are the Olympic Games, the World Cup, the world championships of various sports, the Golden League series and the Grand Prix of athletics, national championships, European cups, etc. Sponsoring events can take the form of financing related to the expenses of the organization or the creation of prize money for the winning athletes or for the athletes achieving records (World Athletics Championships, Golden League, etc.).

IV. Clauses under the Sponsoring Agreement

615. It is a very common phenomenon that the sponsor puts certain clauses in the contract in order to ensure the purpose he seeks with the contract, that is, its promotion to the general public.

616. The most common clauses found in sponsoring contracts are the following.

a. Exclusivity and Non-competition Clause

617. In order for the sponsor to ensure only its own promotion from the receiver's activity and not the parallel promotion of another sponsor, often with a clause in the contract it prohibits the receiver from entering into any other sponsoring contract. Therefore, the question arises as to whether such a clause is legal. At first sight, it seems to conflict with Articles AK 178 and AK 179 as a disadvantage. Thus, for example, one sports goods company could exclude the conclusion of any other sponsorship contract with another sports goods company. After all, anything different would be against the law on unfair competition. Thus, even in the case that this clause is missing, possibly, the second sponsoring contract concluded by the receiver with another sponsor active in the same field of economic activity may be contrary to Article 1 of Law 146/14 on unfair competition.

b. Decent Behaviour Clause

618. This clause is a more specific manifestation of the more general principle of good faith fulfilment of the provision established by the CC 288. Thus, the recipient undertakes the obligation to refrain from negative statements against the recipient and generally refrain from any behaviour that could harm the sponsor. As we have seen, the sponsor aims to enhance the receiver's good reputation, the so-called image, exploiting what he himself will be able to display. In the event that this good reputation changes due to the inappropriate behaviour of the receiver, then the sponsor will not only not benefit from the sponsoring contract, but also the opposite result will occur. Thus, a clause that prohibits the recipient from some extreme behaviours is in principle valid as it is compatible with the very nature and logic of the sponsoring contract. However, such clauses must always be checked with care because they will always be by their very nature at the limits of validity. Thus, in any case, the sponsor could prohibit the recipient from committing criminal acts and certain legal ones that are on the border of morality. However, it could hardly prohibit the performance of legal acts even if they are not the most socially acceptable (e.g., forbidding a young singer from maintaining a relationship with a much older man). In the event that the fair conduct clause is stated in the abstract without further specification, it must be interpreted in that direction.

c. Arbitration and Determination of Applicable Law Clauses

619. Such clauses will usually arise when we have a sponsorship with foreign elements, which is very common in sports sponsorship. Also, it is possible to have an arbitration clause.

620. A sponsoring contract should also contain the following clauses:

- A detailed definition of the exact amount of the financial support and the way it is paid.
- The exact obligations of the receiver of sponsoring. These obligations should be analytically described so that possible future disputes can be avoided.
- An explicit provision for the exact duration of the contract and the conditions for its renewal.
- Clauses protecting the sponsors from the phenomenon of ambush marketing.
- Clauses protecting the athletes' individual rights and their personality and privacy in general.

621. Beyond all the above clauses, it is worth mentioning that the general principles of the CC can always be implemented on sponsorship contracts, whether they have been included in the contract or not.

V. Merchandising

622. The term merchandising is primarily used in marketing to name strivings of the companies for the purpose of improving the rentability of their sales network. Merchandising does not have a long tradition. The roots of its origin belong to the US. Its emergence is closely connected with the increase in the number of products and the creation of big sales objects and primarily refers to the display methods and product representation to increase rentability. In the narrow sense, it implies all activities within the sales space linked to the product itself, such as product positioning and display, promotional activities inside the sales space with the goal of improving sales, etc. Besides its primary use, merchandising refers to the placement on the market of products that contain fictional characters, real persons, personal names, names of sports clubs, etc., or products that use the names and characters of fictional or famous people and elements of art pieces in order to promote and sell the products or services, and all with the goal of exploiting the recognizability of the symbol they represent and with which the consumers wish to identify themselves with (AIPPI, 1995). Merchandising actively contributes to the originality of sales through emotional identification and product presentation, and it combines different material and non-material goods. The indispensable substrate of merchandising is the active building of the trademark since it is exactly the easiest way to emotionally reach the customer and direct the said customer towards a certain product. The elements used in merchandising might be legally protected based on the Law on Trademarks, Law on Authorship, Law on Unfair Competition, and in some countries, even by the act of preventing 'representation of goods of lower quality as the goods of a famous producer'. In the legal sense, merchandising is used to define the rights to use characters or personalities for commercial purposes (Funk, Pizzo, Baker, 2018). Merchandising often also refers to the additional use of intellectual property which generates revenue and often surpasses the revenue acquired through its primary use. The basic form of such transfer of rights is the licence that is characterized by the fact that a certain form of the intellectual property, and most often the brand, is being leased for use on the products that are different from the products for which the said brand was previously created and registered. The contemporary mass media are not only transmitting information but also have, to the contrary, become the main actors of marketing positioning (Vidović & Jugović, 2014). Nowadays, sports objects resemble billboards more than places where sports fans meet. The emission rights or TV rights for certain matches, championships and even the Olympics represent an extremely important segment. The amounts that follow the contracts signed when leasing such rights sometimes surpass the GDP of certain countries.

A. *Character Merchandising*

623. The right to use popular character for commercial purposes is most often manifested in two ways: sometimes the elements of merchandising make the product itself or are applied to the said product, and sometimes they are used only as a propaganda element that is not in any way included in the product. The use of real personalities known to a wider public, that is, personality merchandising, is also called reputation merchandising. The use of images of real personalities is founded in the attitudes of a significant segment of consumers for whom the product itself is not of the primary importance, but the name or the image 'carried' by the said product, and that represents the product's main marketing tool. The use of characteristics of famous personalities is especially widespread in the domain of the entertainment industry (film, television, sport, etc.). The world of contemporary communications offers a wide range of possibilities for processing original works, and thus, many film adaptations of literary works are far more famous than their original works. The legal protection can be enforced through a trademark, authorship rights or stipulations of the unfair competition.

B. Merchandising Trademarks

624. A trademark is a right that protects the stamp that is in traffic used for differentiating goods, that is, services of a natural or a legal person, for the same or similar goods, that is, services provided by some other natural or legal person. The protection of character on the basis of trade mark rights does not demand originality, unlike legal authorship protection that asks for the originality of the work. Moreover, when proving the trade mark copyright infringement, the owner of the rights does not have to prove that the sued entity had access to the character as demanded by the authorship rights, but it is enough to prove that the use was conducted without the permission of the character protected by the trade mark. The duration of a trademark is temporally unlimited since it lasts as long as the protection is being prolonged with the competent authority. Every change in the appearance of the character, however, might harm the original trademark protection, and thus, it often asks for a mandatory supplemental registration (of the new trademark with the said changes) in order to protect the contemporary appearance of the character from unwanted abuse.

C. Merchandising of Sporting Objects

625. Products of sport industry do not anymore include just sports, recreation and fitness activities, material goods and services related to sports, recreation and fitness. The phenomenon that has recently been taking a more and more significant place within the world of merchandising, thanks to, above all, enormous amounts of money that are being invested in it, but also the attention that it causes within the public, is the leasing of rights to naming sporting objects to the sponsor. Sports and entertainment (including music and film) are the most popular forms of social activities that are followed by billions of people worldwide. Because of that, the majority of big global seventy-two producers and service providers are turning their branding strategies to this type of branding. Sponsors that allocate funds in order for a stadium to carry the name of their company or a trademark, besides direct marketing, also wish to achieve an additional synergy expressed through the character of the team played on the said sporting object. The sponsors wish their name to be carried by the stadiums on which plays a team adorned by the traits of their products or the traits they wish their consumers to believe that their products have. Moreover, they count on the fact that ensuring big additional material funds for the functioning of the team causes gratitude and respect among numerous sympathizers and fans of the sponsored club, since in such a way, bigger funds are ensured for the procurement of better and more quality players and coaches. Such contracts are usually concluded for a longer period and sometimes even include other forms of merchandising – above all, writing the names of the sponsors on the sportsmen jerseys. The attention and media promotion acquired through such contracts are huge and represent one of the basic motives for the extremely high financial investments of the sponsors.

626. Intellectual property rights enable legal protection of its key elements: the trademark, the design, authorship, familiar laws, geographic indications of origins and patents. Without intellectual property rights, the life span of successful brands would be limited to months. It provides legal protection and thus enables the preservation of its uniqueness and all the specialities that differentiate it from the variety of similar products or services, thus making it recognizable on the market and enabling its further improvement and economic exploitation through further lease of rights to the use of its different segments.

627. Relevant legislation assisting in protecting and enforcing intellectual property rights in Greece are the laws on Trademarks (Law 4679/2020), Patents (Law 1733/1987), Designs (Law 2417/1996), Copyright and related rights (Law 2121/1993) as currently in force, which include provisions for the enforcement of the relative IP rights. Trademark law and Copyright law also include provisions for the criminal prosecution of trademark and copyright counterfeiting, whereas patent and design counterfeiting do not constitute criminal offences in Greece.

628. Relevant EU-wide provisions are also directly applicable, such as:

- The EU Enforcement Directive 98/71/EP of 13 October 1998 is transposed in the Greek IP laws, but for any issues not transposed, the Enforcement Directive is directly applicable.
- The EU Customs Regulation 608/2013 regulates the grant and enforcement of Applications for Action (AFA) by Greek customs; the Regulation applies for both EU-wide grants of AFAs issued by any EU Customs based on EU IP rights as well as for national grants for AFAs, also based on Greek IP rights.

629. Additionally, a unique and very important tool is the existing specific legislation (comprising laws 4177/2013 and 4712/2020, as currently in force). This legislation enables market controls as well as the seizure and destruction of counterfeit products by a simplified procedure using administrative decisions made by several competent enforcement authorities.

630. The last important legislative changes took place in 2020 with the new Trademarks Law (Law 4679/2020) and the law governing market controls and administrative seizures of counterfeits (Law 4712/2020). These provisions have undergone some changes since their introduction, mostly regarding the procedure of enforcement and seizure of IP rights based on administrative decisions by the competent authorities.

631. Sports law only contains a provision in Article 66, paragraph 2 about the use of the logo of the associations by the AAEs they establish, providing that the AAE must use the emblem or the trademark of the founding sports association and its distinguishing features in its appearance for the matches of her group. The company has the right to use the mark and the distinctive title of the association in any way. This use does not limit the rights of the association to the title, the emblem, the mark and the badges of appearance, which still belong to the association and are freely availed of in all its parts.

632. The AAEs exploit the logo by signing licence agreements with various product manufacturers to produce products (such as clothing, cups, scarfs, balls, etc.) with the logo of the club as well as with companies which undertake the selling of such products through the official stores of the clubs or through internet.

633. Main clauses of those contracts are:

- The Affiliate hereby acknowledges that its right to use the 'Trademark' is limited exclusively to the production and distribution of the products, following the express written consent of the 'Club'.
- The Affiliate is prohibited from substituting another in the use of this licence or granting sublicences (whether of use or of any other kind) or consenting in any way to the use of this licence by a third party without the express written consent of 'CLUB'.
- During the validity of this Agreement, the Affiliate has no right to use any other mark, logo, distinguishing feature or brand which is similar to or may cause confusion with the above mark.
- The trademark, the use of which is hereby granted to the Affiliate, remains in any case the exclusive property of the owner who maintains the right to use it at its sole discretion.
- Products for which the licence to use the trademark is hereby granted are exclusively defined, while the 'Trademark' for which the licence to use is hereby granted is exclusively that shown.
- The Partner undertakes and guarantees compliance with all laws, provisions and safety regulations regarding the manufacture, promotion, distribution and sale of products licensed to bear the trademark, as well as with the relevant instructions of the 'Club'.
- The Partner undertakes the obligation to update at its own expense for the conclusion of this trademark licence agreement the trademark registry pursuant to Article 132 of Law 4072/2012.
- The Partner is obliged to ensure that all products for which it is hereby granted the licence to use the trademark will be of excellent quality, will be safe and suitable for the use for which they are intended, will not be defective and will coincide in all respects with the sample approved by Club.
- The Partner is obliged to ensure that each licensee carries the brand product will have a label, or other similar marking, in accordance with the applicable consumer protection provisions.
- The Partner is also obliged to place on the products licensed to carry the trademark and/or on their packaging and wrappings his name, his address and the country of production in such a way that the consumer is able to distinguish the above data. Ownership of clubs.

634. In the event that a natural or legal person produces and trades products with the group's brand without the required permission from the latter, then the group retains at his expense all rights arising from the trademark and unfair competition provisions. In particular, the emblem of the respective team has been established for many years and is widely recognized both inside and outside football circles, and is used to such an extent that it ended up due to long and continuous use to distinguish, personalize the team and its products and prevailed as a distinguishing characteristic of the group, while with regard to the largest groups in history and popularity, it can be considered as a mark-of-fame now.

635. As a distinguishing feature, it is therefore protected by law 146/1914. Moreover, any falsification and imitation of it by the offending company reasonably creates the risk of confusion for the buying public, constitutes an illegal act and undermines the group's rights to the trademark.

636. In particular, the above violation is provided for under Articles 13–15 of Law 146/1914. The legal consequence of the violation of Article 13 of law 146/1914 is the claim of omission and removal of the insult, which stems directly from the objectively illegal behaviour of the offender. Besides, the offending company, by proceeding to the production and distribution of products bearing the team's emblem, directly violates Article 1 of Law 1146/1914 which provides that any unfair act is also illegal.

637. An essential element for the establishment of a claim for compensation on unfair competition is that the act, which allegedly constitutes unfair competition, is carried out with the intention of competing with the commercial or industrial business carried out by another, as well as being contrary to good faith. An unfair competitive act can also be a tort if the conditions of Articles 914 and 919 of the CC are met, so an additional claim for monetary compensation due to moral damage is not excluded.

VI. Ownership of Clubs

638. As mentioned above (paragraphs 206-214) the sports law contains provisions and limitations on obtaining shares of AAEs.

639. A current international challenge related to club ownership is multi ownership, which came up when huge companies become owners of more than one club in different countries. In principle, this is not prohibited because even sports law in Greece prohibits owning more than one Greek club, but international federations started to include in their regulations provisions to protect the integrity of their competitions.

640. The most characteristic is the example of UEFA which includes in the regulations of its competitions Article 5 which reads as follows:

5.01 To ensure the integrity of the UEFA club competitions (i.e. UEFA Champions League, UEFA Europa League and UEFA Europa Conference League), the following criteria apply:

a. No club participating in a UEFA club competition may, either directly or indirectly:
   i. hold or deal in the securities or shares of any other club participating in a UEFA club competition;
   ii. be a member of any other club participating in a UEFA club competition;
   iii. be involved in any capacity whatsoever in the management, administration and/or sporting performance of any other club participating in a UEFA club competition; or
   iv. have any power whatsoever in the management, administration and/or sporting performance of any other club participating in a UEFA club competition.

b. No one may simultaneously be involved, either directly or indirectly, in any capacity whatsoever in the management, administration and/or sporting performance of more than one club participating in a UEFA club competition.

No individual or legal entity may have control or influence over more than one club participating in a UEFA club competition, such control or influence being defined in this context as:
   i. holding a majority of the shareholders' voting rights;
   ii. having the right to appoint or remove a majority of the members of the administrative, management or supervisory body of the club;
   iii. being a shareholder and alone controlling a majority of the shareholders' voting rights pursuant to an agreement entered into with other shareholders of the club; or
   iv. being able to exercise by any means a decisive influence in the decision-making of the club.

5.02 If two or more clubs fail to meet the criteria aimed at ensuring the integrity of the competition, only one of them may be admitted to a UEFA club competition, in accordance with the following criteria (applicable in descending order):

a. the club which qualifies on sporting merit for the most prestigious UEFA club competition (i.e., in descending order: UEFA Champions League, UEFA Europa League or UEFA Europa Conference League);
b. the club which was ranked highest in the domestic championship giving access to the relevant UEFA club competition;
c. the club whose association is ranked highest in the access list (*see* Annex A).

5.03 Clubs that are not admitted are replaced in accordance with Paragraph 4.09.

5.04 This article is not applicable if any of the cases listed under Paragraph 5.01 happens between a club directly qualified to the UEFA Champions League group stage and one qualified for any stage of the UEFA Europa Conference League.

§3. Epilogue

641. Sports law is a section of law science under continuous development worldwide. In Greece though it is still in the early stages. The necessity for sports law to be included in the lessons planning of law and physical education in university schools is obvious. This work included in the International Encyclopedia of Laws aims to put a stone in this effort.

Selected Bibliography

Agioutanis, G., G. Kabouroglou & N. Gartanos. 'Doping – Public Conversation, Symposium of the Sport – Medical Society'. *Sport Medicine* 5, no. 7 (1968): 7.

Anagnostopoulos, H. *Capabilities and Limits of Penal Legislation for Sport Violence – Minutes of the European Congress for the Confrontation of Violence in Sport Fields*, 17–19 February 1989, 172.

Anagnostopoulos, H. *The Unprovoked Crimes – A Comprehensive Interpretation.* NoB 1986, 359.

Andreou, F. *Civil Prosecution in Penal Trial.* Larisa, 1999.

Androulakis, N. *About Concurrence of Crimes.* A' 1966, B' 1968.

Androulakis, N. *Clash: Art. 313 PC.* Pen.Min ΚΔ, 1974, 481.

Androulakis, N. *Elements of Bribery. – Offers Due to Social Reasons.* PinChron ΛΘ, 1989, 635.

Androulakis, N. *Fundamental Notions of Penal Trial.* A, B, C, 1994.

Androulakis, N. *Malpractice – Unwritten Capital Element of the Crime of Malpractice.* PinChron KE, 1975, 161.

Androulakis, N. *Nullum crimen sine lege certa.* Pen.Min ΚΓ, 1973, 513.

Androulakis, N. *Penal Law – General Part.* Athens: Sakkoulas, 2000.

Androulakis, N. *Penal Law.* Special Part, Sakkoulas, 1974.

Androulakis, N. *Penal Studies*, 1972.

Androulakis, N. *The Meaning of Violence in Penal Law.* PinChron I ΙΓ, 1963, 593.

Antonopoulos, B. *Law of Commercial Societies.* Sakkoulas, 1997.

Arvanitis, G. *Concurrence of Bribery and False Certification.* Pen.Min K, 1970, 240.

Astrinakis, A. & L. Stilianoudis. *Heavy Metal, Rockabili, Fans*, 1996.

Bek Karolos. *Olympic Games 1896.* Athens, 1996.

Bekas, G. *Weapons, Explosives, Ammunition*, 1995.

Bitzilekis, N. *Remarks on A.P. 1092/1995*, Def. 1995, 1135.

Bitzilekis, N. *The Participating Act.* Thessaloniki, 1990.

Bitzilekis, N. *The Service Crimes.* Thessaloniki, 2001.

Bomis, A. *Goal 2000, One Century of Football.* Athens, 2000.

Bondoux, R. *Sport and Law – Minutes of the International Olympic Academy, 18th SDOA.* Athens, 1978, 174.

Bowman, S. & X. Tsorbatzoudis. *Psychology in Sport.* Thessaloniki, 1998.

Charalambakis, A. *The Financial Crimes in Sport, – Minutes of B' Legal Congress Justice and Sport*, 18–19 April 1997, Sakkoulas, 49.

Chatziharistos, D. *Modern System of Physical Education.* Athens, 1990.

Selected Bibliography

Chorafas, N. *General Principles of Penal Law*, 1964.

Chorafas, N. *Special Part 1945, Penal Law*. Care of Publication K. Stamatis, Athens: Sakkoulas, 1978.

Christodoulatos, Ch. *EFIP and Sport Disciplinary Law – Proceedings of 1st IASL Congress on Sport Law*. Athens, 1993, 448.

Christodoulatos, Ch. *The Work of EFIP*. IOC, 1985.

Christodoulou, K. *Sports Law*. Athens: Nomiki Vivliothiki, 2023

Dedes, H. *Penal Proceedings*, 1989.

Deligiannis, I. & B. Skouris. *Legal Nature of the Sport Judge and Legitimacy of His Disciplinary Power – Giving of Opinion*. Armenopoulos, 1986, 580.

Demetratos, N. *Legal Good and Lessons about Crime in Penal Law*, 1998.

Dimou, N. *Introduction, Minutes of B' Legal Congress Justice and Sport*, 18–19 April 1997, 109.

Dionisatos S. & K. Dris. T*he Legal Nature of Sport Judge – Proceedings 1st IASL Congress on Sport Law*. Athens, 1993, 383.

Dionisatos, G. *Sport Disputes and the Right for Judicial Protection*. Pandektis 1992, 85.

Dionisatos, S. *What is the Importance of EFIP Nowadays, Sport Disputes*. Sport Law Review 2, 1996, 109.

Dotsas, P. *Medicines and Olympic Spectacle*. Thessaloniki: University Studio Press, 1995.

Dtzioras, D. *Book of Special Penal Law*. First Part, V. A' 1971.

Erantos, K. *Sport and Society*. Thessaloniki, 1990.

Falkos-Arvanitakis, A. *The Greek Sport*. Volos, 2003.

Farandos, G. *Problems of Ethic in Sport, Aggression and Violence, Sport Psychology*, 1986, 8.

Farandos, G. *Theory of the Science of Sport Law, Proceedings 1st IASL Congress on Sport Law*. Athens, 1993, 43.

Fefes, M. *The Sport Behaviour in the Last 50 Years: Legal Dimensions, Fan in the 21st Century*. Athens, 2000, 63.

Filippidis, T. *Bribery Thanks to Legal Acts*. Honorary Volume H. Kyriakopoulou, 1966–1969, 903.

Filippidis, T. *Lessons of Penal Law*. Special Part, V. A', Publ. Sakkoulas 1979, V. B', 1981.

Filippidis, T. *The Consent of the Victim*, 1951.

Filippidis, T. *The Penal Liability of the Legal Entities*, 1950.

Flegas, K. *The Legal Position of the 'Professional' Amateur Athletes in Greek Legal Order*. Sport and Law 2023/1, 55.

Frantzeskakis, I. *Antisocial Behaviour of the Youth, Hooliganism*. Anarchy, Terrorism, Drugs, Athens – Komotini: A. Sakkoulas, 1987.

Fronimos, E. *Notion of Clash of Art. 313 PC*. NoB, 1965, 346.

Gafos, H. *Penal Law*. General Part, V. A'–C' 1973–1978.

Gafos, H. *Penal Law*. Special Part, V. A' 1957, V. B' 1959, V. C' 1961, V. D' 1963, V. E' 1965, V. F' 1967, V. G' 1969.

Gafos, H. *Penal Proceedings*, 1966.

Gafos, H. *The Crime of Bribery*. PinChron I, 1960, 341.

Gargalianos, D. & Avgerinos Th. *The Organization of Sport in International Level.* Annual International Review I, 243.
Gavrielides, A., *Body Damage of Children*, etc., Art. 312 PC, 1975.
Georgakis, I. *Penal Law General Part,* 1960.
Georgakis, I. *Penal Law General Part.* Athens – Komotini: Sakkoulas, 1991.
Giakoumelos, S. *Sport Legislation and Jurisprudence.* Athens, 2000.
Giannakis, Th., *History of Physical Education and of Sport During the Roman and the Byzantine Empire.* Athens, 1978.
Giannakis, Th., *History of Physical Education.* Athens, 1990.
Giannopoulos, Th., *The Penal Suppression in Front of the Particularities of the Phenomenon of Violence in Sport Fields, Minutes of the European Congress for the Confrontation of Violence in Sport Fields.* Athens, 17–19 February 1989, 180.
Giatsis, S. *Introduction in the History of Physical Education.* Thessaloniki, 1985.
Goulas, D. *Employment Relationship of Athletes.* Thessaloniki: Sakkoulas, 2014.
Houlihan, B. *Doping, Papazisi.* Athens, 1999.
Hrysogonos, K. *Individual and Social Rights.* Thessaloniki, 2002.Kaiafa – Gbanti, M. *External and Internal Negligence.* Thessaloniki, 1994.
Kaiafa – Gbanti, M. *Penal Law in 2000: Looking at the Future Without Thinking about the Past.* Def. 200, 47.
Kalavros, K. *Competence of Civil Courts for Sport Disputes.* NoB, 1986, 532.
Karanikas, D. *Book of Penal Law.* Special Part, V. B' 1954, V. C' 1962.
Karras, A. *Penal Proceedings.* Publ. B' Sakkoulas, 1998.
Kastrinos, Th. *Sport as Public Danger.* Athens, 1999.
Katsantonis, A. *Penal Law.* General Part, V. A' 1972, V. B' 1978.
Kesaris, P. *About the Provision of Article 61 paragraph 3 law 75/1975.* Pen.Min ΚΘ, 1979, 524.
Konstantaras, D. & M. Kontoleon. *Glory and Tear.* Patakis, Athens, 2000.
Koukiadis I. & N. Nikas. *Jurisprudence Issues Arising during the Procedure of Examination of Sport Disputes by EEODAK/ESAKE.* Armenopoulos, 2003, 911.
Koulouris A. & X. Tsouramanis. *Hooliganism, Opinions about a Modern Problem – Theoretical Approach.* Sport Science, 1986, 7.
Kourakis N. & Partners. *Report about the Violence in the Greek Fields, Conclusions Out of Seven Different Researches and General Conclusions, Honorary Volume to the Honour of Helias Daskalakis*, 1992, 299.
Kourakis, N. *Violence in Greek Fields between Theory and Reality – Minutes of B' Legal Congress of Justice and Sport*, 18–19 April 1997, 153.
Kousoulis S. & A. Malatos. *Sport Legislation.* Athens 2003.
Koutselinis, A. *Doping Brief Presentation of the Problem.* Parisianos, Athens, 1986.
Kranidiotis, P. *The Psychological Reasons for Doping.* Athletic Psychology, 1984, 5.
Kritikos, A. *Law of Associations and Syndicates.* Athens 1984.
Leontaris, M. *Limited Companies.* Pamissos, 2000.
Lianos, G. *Sport Civil Liability.* Sport and Law, 2023/1, 3
Lianos, G. *Sport Self Administration.* Athens: Nomiki Vivliothiki, 2020.
Liaros, D. & D. Panagiotopoulos. 'Doping, Anti-sporting Behaviour. The Disciplinary and Penal Side of the Problem'. *Review of Sport Law* 1 (1994): 173.

Selected Bibliography

Liaros, D. *The Penal Dimension of Anti-sporting Behaviour, Proceedings of 1st IASL Congress on Sport Law*. Athens, 1993, 285.

Liourdis, A. *Managing of Other's Property and Malpractice According to Article 390 PC*. PinChron MD, 1994, 722.

Livos, N. *About Group Insults*. PinChron MA, 1991, 1217.

Loverdos, A. *The Protection of Sport as an Individual and Social Good – Proceedings 1st IASL Congress on Sport Law*. Athens, 1993, 171.

Magakis, G.A. *Penal Law*. General Part, Athens, 1981.

Magakis, G.A. *Penal Law*. Layout of General Part, Papazisi, Athens, 1982.

Magganas, A. *About Hooliganism, Penal Law,* 1998, 566.

Malatos A. & K. Mantaios. *Public Policy Against Sport Violence*. Rev. Sp.L., 1993, 20.

Malatos, A. *Introduction in Sport Law*. The Sport Legal Order, Rev. Sp.L., 1992, 175.

Malatos, A. *Judicial Control of Disciplinary Power on Sport*. NoB, 1987, 1497.

Malatos, A. *Scientific Approach of Sport Law*. Athens, 2000.

Malatos, A. *Sport and European Legal Order after the Bosman Decision*. Athens, 1996.

Malatos, A. *Sport Justice: Meaning, Goal, Structure, Function*. Rev. Sp.L., 1994, 12.

Malatos, A. *Sport Law Lessons*, Athens-Komotini, 2005.

Manitakis A. & A. Anastasiades. *The Greek Constitution*. Thessaloniki: Giannopoulos, 1984.

Manolaros, F. *Valid Sport Legislation and Judicial Practice – Minutes of B' Legal Congress of Justice and Sport.* 18–19 April 1997, 138.

Manoledakis, I. & T. Filippidis. *Opinion*. Arm. 1980, 875.

Manoledakis, I. *Interpretation of the Art. of the Special Part of the Penal Code*, 1996.

Manoledakis, I. *Penal Law*. General Part, Thessaloniki: Sakkoulas, 1985, 1999.

Manoledakis, I. *Studies for Deepening in the Penal Law 1990*, 1995.

Manoledakis, I. *The Dialectic Notion of Legal Goods*. Thessaloniki: Sakkoulas, 1973.

Manoledakis, I. *The Legal Good as a Basic Notion of the Penal Law*. Thessaloniki: Sakkoulas, 1998.

Manoledakis, I. *Threat Against the Public Order*. Thessaloniki, 1994.

Manoledakis, I. *Violations Against the Public Power*. Thessaloniki, 1988.

Maragou, I. *Violations of Provisions of the Special Part of the Greek Penal Code Resulted from Sport Meetings of the Sport Seasons of 1992–1993*, Review of Sport Law 2, 1996, pp. 87, etc.

Margaritis, L. & N. Paraskevopoulos. *About Penalties*. Sakkoulas, 1991, 1995.

Margaritis, L. *Body Injuries, Sakkoulas, Thessaloniki 1991 – Remarks on Juridical Decision of Larissa 171/1992*. Def. 1992, 1461.

Mavromatis, A. *Penal Crimes in Sport*. PhD, Thessaloniki, 2002.

Mavromatis, A. *Sport and Penal Law, Introductive – Dogmatic Approach*. Pen. Just. 2005, 1323.

Mavromatis, A. *Sport Crimes*. Sakkoulas, 2006.

Mavromatis, A. *Sport Ethic and Application of Penal and Disciplinary Law for Violent Behaviour in the Field of Sport*. Armenopoulos, 2004, 439.
Mihail, K. *Marginalization of Youth and Post War Forms of Juvenile Delinquency. Their Legal Confrontation then and Now*. Arm. 1987, 203.
Milonopoulos, X. *Crimes Distinguished by their Result*, 1984.
Ministry of Sport. *General Secretariat of Sport, Greek Sport – Historic Review*. Athens, 1998.
Morris, D. *The Football Tribe*. Athens: Cactos, 1982.
Nafziger, J. *International Sport Law*. translation by K. Chatzikonstadinou, Thessaloniki, 1991.
Naskou – Perraki, P. & D. Panagiotopoulos. *Sport: Texts of International Practice*. Athens – Komotini, 1993.
Naskou – Perraki, P. *International Institutions Law I, Institutional Dimension*. Athens – Komotini: A. Sakkoulas, 1989.
Naskou – Perraki, P. *The European Convention about Violence and Misbehaviour of Spectators During the Sport Events and Especially the Football Games*. in *Sport Psychology,* 1987.
Nikolaidou, E. & X. Katsikas. *Olympic Games in Ancient Greece, The Non Visible Aspects*, Athens, 2003.
Nisireos, E. *Business Risk and the Crime of Malpractice*. NoB, 1991, 1064.
Oplantzakis, B. *Introduction in the Problematic of Doping*. Rev. Sp.L., 1992, 213.
Paleologos, Kl. *Genesis, Foundation and Evolution of the Olympic Games in Antiquity*. IOC, 2nd Meeting, Anc. Olympia, 1962.
Pamboukis, K. *Commercial Societies Law*. Sakkoulas, 1979.
Panagiotopoulos, D. *Categories of Torts in Sport Activity and Definition of Liabilities*. NoB, 2000, 1377.
Panagiotopoulos, D. *Doping – Legal Confrontation*. Sakkoulas, 1991.
Panagiotopoulos, D. *Law of International Sport Relations and Institutions*. Athens: Sakkoulas, 1995.
Panagiotopoulos, D. *Law of the Olympic Games, Institutional Framework in Ancient Greece and in Modern Times*. Athens – Komotini: Sakkoulas, 1991.
Panagiotopoulos, D. *Legal Confrontation of Violence in Sport*. Penal Justice 2012, 145.
Panagiotopoulos, D. *Review of Sport Law 1: Right to Sport*. Athens – Komotini: Sakkoulas, 1994.
Panagiotopoulos, D. *Review of Sport Law 2: Sport Disputes*. Athens – Komotini: Sakkoulas, 1996.
Panagiotopoulos, D. *Review of Sport Law 3: Sport Activity as Profession*. Athens – Komotini: Sakkoulas, 1997.
Panagiotopoulos, D. *Sport Association*. Athens: Nomiki Vivliothiki, 2022.
Panagiotopoulos, D. *Sport Jurisdiction*. Athens – Komotini: Sakkoulas, 1997.
Panagiotopoulos, D. *Sport Law as Sport of the Administration and the Organization of Sport, of Regulation of the Sport Relations and the Sport Disputes*. Adm. Just., 1991, 20.
Panagiotopoulos, D. *Sport Law, First Systematical Approach and Scientific Grounding*. Athens, 2000.
Panagiotopoulos, D. *Sport Law, Systematic View – Application*. Legal Library, 2005.

Selected Bibliography

Panagiotopoulos, D. *Sport Law: Scientific Approach*. Pandektis 1/1992, 25.

Panagiotopoulos, D. *Sport Quality*. Athens – Komotini: Sakkoulas, 1990.

Panagiotopoulos, D. *The Doping Problem – Precaution and Suppression Measures*. Sport Science, EKAE 1992, 9.

Panagiotopoulos, D. *Theory of Sport Law*. Athens – Komotini, 1990.

Panagopoulos, G. *General Review of Sport Justice in Greece*. Rev. Sp.L., 1992, 337.

Panousis, I. *Hooliganism: A Social Phenomenon with Two Faces*. Sport Psychology, 1987, 39.

Panousis, I. *Is the Violent Fan a Real Fan? Fan in the 20th Century*, 2000, 17.

Panousis, I. *Opinions about Sport Violence*. Athens – Komotini: Sakkoulas, 1990.

Papadakis, B. *Special Penal Law*, V. B'.

Papadamakis, A. *Insults Against the International State Existence*, 1995.

Papadamakis, A. *Property Crimes*. Athens – Thessaloniki: Sakkoulas, 2000.

Papadamakis, A. *Remarks on A.P. 420/1998*. Def. 1999, 1080.

Papadatos, P. *Aggression, Violence and Destructions Within the Social Life*, 1980.

Papadogiannakis, I. *Doping as a Penal Act – Proceedings 1st IASL Congress on Sport Law*, 302.

Papadogiannakis, I. *Doping in Sport – Minutes B' Legal Congress Sport and Justice*. Sakkoulas, 18–19 April 1997, 57.

Papadogiannis, M. *About Crimes of Doping and Violation of the Security of Transport*. PinChron IST, 1966, 573.

Papaharalambous, X. *The Unprovoked Criminality: Structure and Prospectives of a Legal Form*. PinChron MH, 1998, 17.

Papakonstantinou, I. *Penal Acts During a Sport Event – Minutes B' Legal Congress Sport and Justice*. Sakkoulas, 18–19 April 1997, 67.

Papaloukas, M. *Doping,* 1995.

Papaloukas, M. *Doping, the Law of State and the Regulations of the Sport Institutions,* Review of Sport Law 2, 1996, 99.

Papaloukas, M. *European Sports Market*. Athens, 2012.

Papaloukas, M. *The Release of Athlete from Criminal Liability for Sport Injuries*. Penal Justice, 2011, 367.

Papaloukas, M. *The Role of State and of the Sport Institutions in the Legal Confrontation of Doping – Proceedings 1st IASL Congress on Sport Law*, 313.

Papasiopi – Pasia, Z. *Citizenship Law*. Sakkoulas, 1987.

Papasteriou, D. *General Principles of Civil Law*. Sakkoulas, 1998.

Paraskevopoulos, N. *Belief and Liability in Penal Law*, 1987.

Paraskevopoulos, N. *Penal Liability from Self – Destructive Acts*. EllEpEgl, 1989, 3–4, 58.

Paraskevopoulos, N. *The Suppression of the Spreading of Drugs in Greece*. Thessaloniki, 1997.

Paraskevopoulos, N. *The Suppression of Use of Drugs in Greece*, 1989.

Pavlou, S. *Interpretation of Law about Drugs*, 1998.

Perakis, E. *The New Law for the Limited Companies*. Athens: Nomiki Vivliothiki, 2019.

Pentzias, G. *Penal Trial*. Athens, 1993.

Pilz, G. *New Tendencies in the Confrontation of Hooliganism, Minutes of the European Congress for the Confrontation of Violence in Sport Fields*. Athens, 17–19 February 1989, 29.

Piperopoulos, G. *A Psychologist in the Sport Field*, 1985.

Piperopoulos, G. *Anatomy of Violence, Physical Education and Sport*, 1988, 50.

Poulis, G. *Contribution to the Interpretation of the Term 'Shameful Act' of Art. 353 PC*. Arm. 1978, 371.

Psarouda – Benaki, A. *The Civil Prosecution in Penal Trial, 1982, Opinion*. PinChron ΛΘ, 1989, 146.

Psarouda – Benaki, A. *The Crime of the Dangerous Body Injury*. PinChron, 1976, 433.

Remelis, K. *Legal Nature of Disciplinary Sport Disputes*. Arm. 1994, 101.

Remelis, K. *Notion and Nature of Sport Disputes – Proceedings 1st IASL Congress on Sport Law*. Athens, 1993, 171.

Reppas, X. *Disputes in the Ancient Olympics, History 142*, 1980, 12.

Rime, B. & M. Dumamand. *Psycho-Sociological Analysis of Violence in the Football Fields and Conclusions We Can Make*. University of Louvain, Belgium 1985, in Athletic Psychology, 1986.

Rontogiannis, G. *Allowed Pharmaceutical Substances to Athletes*. Sport Science, 1991, 17.

Rontogiannis, G. *Health Problems of Olympic Athletes*. Hippocrates 4, 1991, 23.

Rontogiannis, G. *Pharmaceutical Substances and Methods Prohibited to Athletes*. Sport Science, 1990, 92.

Rontogiannis, G. *Undesired Effects of Doping on Athletes*. Sport Science 1988, 151.

Simeonidou – Kastanidou, E. *Penal Law*, Special Part. Athens – Komotini: 4th publ. Sakkoulas, 1999.

Simeonidou – Kastanidou, E. *The Crime of Illegal Violence According to Article 330 PC*. Arm. 1982, 972.

Simeonidou – Kastanidou, E. *The Violence against a Third Person in the Crime of Resistance*. PinChron ΛΕ, 1985, 189.

Skalides, L. *Commercial Societies Law*. Jus, 1993.

Skiadas, E. *100 Years of Modern Olympic History, Committee of Olympic Games – The News*. Athens, 1996.

Spiliopoulos, X. *Medicines Used in Doping and Undesired Effects of them, 1st Symposium, Prevention and Modern Therapy of Sport Damages*. Athens, 1990.

Spinellis, D. *Insult with Group Characterization*. PinChron KZ, 1977, 917.

Spinellis, D. *Penal Law Special Part, Crimes Against Honour,* 1980.

Spinellis, D. *Penal Law Special Part, Crimes against Property Goods*, V. A' 1984, V. B' 1985.

Spinellis, D. *Penal Law Special Part: Service Crimes*, 1988.

Spinellis, D. *Penalties in Legal Entities and Procedure of their Infliction*. PinChron ΝΓ, 2003, 97.

Spinellis, D. *Problems from Crimes of Risk*. PinChron ΚΓ, 1973, 161.

Spinellis, D. *The Legal Good and Its Importance in the Modern Teaching of Penal Law*. PinChron KA, 1971, 721, etc.

Spyrakos, D. *The Critical Function of the Notion of Legal Good*. Athens, 1996.

Spyrakos, D. *The Penal Liability of Enterprises, Development or Violation of Penal Law*. PinChron MΔ, 1994, 1201.
Stamatis, K. *About Body Injury on Children*. PinChron KΔ, 1974, 714.
Stamatis, K. *General Principles of the Fake Concurrence of Crimes, Committed with One Act*, 1972.
Stamatis, K. *The Concurrence of Penal Laws in General and the Non-punishable Previous or a Posteriori Act*, 1967.
Stamatis, K. *The Notion of the Result Crime*. PinChron IΔ, 1964, 188.
Stamiris, I. *Sociology of Sport and Sport*, University of Athens, 1987.
Statheas, G. *Interpretation of the New Law about Drugs*, 1988.
Stathopoulos, M. *Issues of Procedure and Normal Law Concerning Sport Disputes, Opinion*. NoB, 1986, 528.
Stathopoulos, M. *Sport and European Community Law – Proceedings 5th IASL Congress*. Nafplio, 1997, 23.
Sylikos, G. *The Materiality of Legal Goods in the Penal Law*. Athens, 1996.
Szwarc, A. *Doping in Sport under the Point of View of Polish Penal Law*. transl. A. Malatou, Rev. Sp.L., 1992, 497.
Tambakis, A. *Judicial Settlement of Sport Disputes – Proceedings 1st IASL Congress on Sport Law*. Athens, 1993, 358.
Tambakis, A. *Offer of Sport Services. Sport Law in the 21st Century, EKEAD*. Athens, 1999, 423.
Tambakis, A. *Working Sport Contracts*. DEN, 1994, 1061.
Tandopoulos, A. *The Problem of Doping in Athletes*. Medicine, 1981, 81.
Travlos, A. *Aggression and Violence in Sport: Family, Education, Mass Media. Sport Law in the 21st Century: Sport Activity as Profession – Minutes of 1st Congress of Sport Law with International Participation*. Trikala, 4–6.6.1999, 315.
Travlos, A. *Spectators-Fans-Hooligans, Sport Notion, Profile and Violent Behaviour, Sport in the 21st Century*, 2000, 39.
Tsarouhas, P. *Anti-doping Control and its Methodology*. Stadion, 1990, 73.
Tsitsoura, A. *The Prevention and the Suppression of Corruption (bribery) in the Frame of Anti-Criminal Policy.* The Penal Convention of the Council of Europe, PenJust, 2000, 875.
Tsoukala, A. *The Policy of the European Instruments Against Hooliganism and its Effects on the Greek Law*. Def. 1995, 399.
Tsouramanis, Ch. *The Behavior of Hooligans*. Athens: Sakkoulas, 1988.
Tsouramanis, Ch. *The Confrontation of Violence in the Greek Sport Fields, Proceedings 1st Congress on Sport Law, EKEAD*. Athens, 1993, 293.
Tsoutsas, N. *About the Abolition or Not of Article 62 paragraph 2 of law 75/1975 'About Out of School Sport'*. PinChron ΛΔ, 1984, 972.
Tzortzopoulos. *Book of Penal Law*, V. 1, 1936.
Venizelos, E. *Sport and State of Justice, the Limits of the Legal Derangement and Return to the Constitution, Minutes of the 1st International Congress of Sport Law*. Athens, 1992, EKEAD.
Venizelos, E. *The Constitutional Reception of Sport, Minutes of the International Congress: The Institution of the Olympic Games*. Olympia 1991, 269 and Pandektis 1, 1992, 212.

Vlastos, S. *Civil Associations – Syndicate and Employers Organizations*. Athens, 1999.
Vougioukas, K. *Financial Penal Law*. 5th publ., 1986.
Vougioukas, K. *Penal Law of Legal Procedure*. 6th publ., Sakkoulas, 1984.
Voultsis, I. *The Strict Liability in Disciplinary Sport Law, Proceedings 1st IASL Congress on Sport Law*. Athens, 1993, 384.
Wolfgang M. & F. Ferracuti. *The Subculture of Violence*, 1996.
Zambelis, G. *Hooligans and Kamikazi*, 1990.
Zagklis, A. *Employment Relationship of Athletes in Professional and Amateur Sport*. DEN 2005, 318.
Zervas, G. *Aggression and Violence in Sport*. Rev. Sp.L., 1993, 11.
Zikopoulos, E. *The Lethal Injury as a Crime after Result*. Arm. 1977, 67.
Zisiades, B. *The Crime as Completed and the Attempt of a Crime,* 1970.
Zisiades, I. *Penal Law.* General Part, V. A' 1971.
Zisiades, I. *Penal Proceedings*. three volumes, 1976.
Zisiades, I. *Sport and Penal Law*, 1944.
Zisiades, I. *Sport Crimes*, Dikastiki 9, 1937, 190, republished in Rev. Sp.L., 1992, 195.

Selected Bibliography

Index

The numbers here refer to paragraph numbers.

Index

www.ingramcontent.com/pod-product-compliance
Lightning Source LLC
Chambersburg PA
CBHW070250030525
26096CB00033B/1337
9789403524184